Deferred Admission

Stories from a kid who skipped college to move to China and work for a Bitcoin billionaire

Bill Byrne

Although the publisher and the author have made every effort to ensure that the information in this book was correct at press time, and while this publication is designed to provide accurate information in regard to the subject matter covered, the publisher and the author assume no responsibility for errors, inaccuracies, omissions, or any other inconsistencies herein and hereby disclaim any liability to any party for any loss, damage, or disruption caused by errors or omissions, whether such errors or omissions result from negligence, accident, or any other cause.

Copyright © 2020 Bill Byrne
All rights reserved.
ISBN-13: 9798555762078

for my parents

Contents

1	China on a Whim	1
2	Getting the Job - Moving to Shanghai	8
3	Crypto Primer	17
4	First Taste of Things to Come	22
5	Finally, Gaining Momentum	26
6	Taiwanese Supermodels Sell Internet Scam Money	32
7	Road Trip	37
8	Decadence	46
9	Michael's Now a Crypto Billionaire	52
10	Chinese Billionaires Buy Me Lunch	53
11	I Live in the Airport	58
12	Trouble from the Valley	61
13	National Lampoon's CNY Vacation – Cambodia	67
14	Stress Dreams	76
15	Oligarchs, Diamonds, and Bankers – Mauritius	79
16	Interim – March in Shanghai	90

17	Closing Bell – Back in Tokyo	94
18	Cracks Begin to Show	102
19	Lashing Out	108
20	It's Been a Slow Year	123
21	New York – A New Start	129
22	European Vacation	137
23	Tired of Taipei	147
24	Afterword: You Can Try This at Home	151

This book is a memoir. Names have been altered and the chronology condensed for the sake of storytelling. Incidents and details are described as I experienced them or as they were relayed to me at the time.

Chapter 1

China on a Whim

"Seriously, how could I possibly think that was a good idea?"

When I was 17, I decided to skip college and move, by myself, to Shanghai. Since then I've done business all across the world, made (and lost) hundreds of thousands of dollars in minutes, bribed Cambodian soldiers, met with African oligarchs, and scammed Russians. I've sipped tea with Chinese gangsters and rap stars, partied with Taiwanese politicians and supermodels, and blacked out in Tokyo's underground clubs. I've been a good guy, been a shithead, become fluent in Chinese, and handled a home invasion committed by some pretty bad people, after which I had to go on the run. I got married and am now a soon-to-be father. I turn 21 tomorrow.

Within two weeks of graduating high school, I moved to China on a whim and a loose promise of a summer internship. The original expectation was to return to America within two months and pursue the traditional path of college and career, but the first year passed quickly without a single visit home. Now, three years later, I have experienced more than I thought I would in an 80-year lifespan.

Deferred Admission

I did not expect or plan for any of this, but looking back on it, it doesn't surprise me either.

It all stems from my deep hatred of school. I wish I could say I appreciated being introduced to things like Russian literature in high school, but I wasn't allowed to read Tolstoy just to read Tolstoy. Instead, I was dictated a choice of which "lens" I would understand it through: feminism or Marxism. What a coincidence. I hated how my scholastic success was heavily based on how well I could regurgitate the teacher's progressive interpretation of *The Kreutzer Sonata*. Zealous late-twenty-something teachers armed with master's degrees, giddy over their control of a room of kids. But I digress…

Needless to say, I got in trouble frequently, and when I did, I'd double down. If the school tried to exert authority over me, I'd triple down — and go on the offensive. I refused to submit and only got more belligerent with time. Fortunately, I had supportive parents, and a school has limited recourse when your parents are willing to back you.

For me, the most important instance of this occurred in my senior year. All of my graduation requirements had been fulfilled in the fall of my senior year, per the rules of my state. But my school pushed extra requirements on its students that went beyond a simple state diploma. My parents saw that I was agitated and bored and agreed to petition the school to consider letting me skip out on the second half of the year. The school didn't say yes, but they didn't say no either. Instead they allowed me some leniency on the condition that I'd do something constructive with the free time. This was easy for me. I had already been working on personal business projects, at the expense of school effort, since my sophomore year. Friends and I opened a virtual office in Panama to run a sportsbook arbitrage business, tried to get into stock trading, and most recently had gotten involved in the cryptocurrency market. We were designing our own cryptocurrency business, and I was already getting up hours before school to work on the project and take overseas conference calls. The only thing limiting the constructive use of my time was school itself.

Sophomore year was also the start of frequent family excursions to Asia. My dad traveled there several times a year for work and wanted the whole family to be involved. My first trip ever, in 2015, was a quick five-night sprint through Beijing and Tokyo. I was hooked on China instantly, already abruptly over-stimulated as I looked out the window on descent into Beijing. I think this addiction to the feeling of hyper-foreignness is common, I see it in all the travel vloggers. Anyway, people tend to have a very immediate love/hate reaction to China, and I loved it. Tokyo, on the other hand, didn't particularly interest me. It would be wrong to say it doesn't feel foreign, or that it's too "Western", but whatever feeling of foreignness it does have doesn't hit you quite as violently as the experience of Beijing on your first time outside of the United States. Over the course of the rest of high school, my family went to China and other Asian destinations every few months when we had sufficient school breaks. Seoul, Singapore, Bangkok… they were all fine, but every chance I got I directed family travel back to China.

Another one of the places we enjoyed was Taipei, which at the time rivaled Beijing as my favorite city. We joked that if Tokyo and Beijing had a baby, it would be called Taipei. Not much of a joke once I realized that's essentially what Taipei is. When deciding what to do with the second half of senior year, we came up with the idea of moving the family to Taipei so I could study Chinese full time, while also continuing to tinker with my business plans.

We didn't realize that temporarily moving to Taipei to study Chinese would mark the end of my life in America. It was the beginning of a series of surreal events, ever increasing in intensity, that had me in a near unbroken state of disbelief. This sense was so pervasive that eventually I could no longer be phased — or more than marginally excited — by anything. The first instance of this was the actual move to Taipei. Honestly, just being there instead of school was exhilarating. Learning Chinese was my immediate job and I scheduled it so my lessons were interchangeable with exploring the city and working on my business.

On the business end, I quickly discovered that there were lots of people interested in cryptocurrency in Taipei, and they had pretty large meetup groups. I reached out to the largest group and told them I was in town, working on a crypto project. They invited me to come present to a meetup they were having the next week. It was an amazing offer, but I didn't have any formal presentation prepared. I called my friend/business partner and convinced him to fly out to Taipei during his finals week and help improvise the presentation.

This was the second notable *wow/Jesus/can't believe this* moment of note. I felt like such a f*cking hot shot. It is easy to get worked up over presenting the fruits of your hobby to other hobbyists if you mentally phrase it as being "invited to speak internationally on cryptocurrency markets." Although back then, everyone and their mother who had any involvement in crypto was "invited to speak internationally." I feel my excitement is excusable since I was 17, but lots of 30-year-olds added that to their resumes that year.

Overhyped or not, it was a step in the right direction of taking action and gaining momentum. My partner showed up after 20 hours of travel and we went straight to work — almost. Drinking age isn't enforced for white people in Asia, so before our speech we had a couple drinks, then very nervously presented our business plans to a room of Taiwanese adults. We were surprisingly well received, exchanged contact information with interested people, gave an interview to the media, then made a beeline for the nearest expat bar to indulge ourselves. We barhopped until around 2 a.m., celebrating our new lives as teenage international business executives, then went back to our apartment so my friend could sleep before his 7 a.m. flight back to the US. His first trip to Asia had lasted a whole 30 hours, barely more than the amount of time he spent flying round trip.

A day or two later, one of the people I'd exchanged contact info with reached out, asking to meet about potential for cooperation with his company. I met the guy at a coffee shop and he talked my ear off for around three hours. I didn't see any potential, but I told him I'd be going to Shanghai in a week before I returned to the US for high school graduation. If he knew anyone involved in crypto there, an introduction would be much appreciated. He said he'd think about it and let me know. At the time I felt like the meeting had been a total waste, but it was actually of unimaginable importance.

He sent me a contact the next day on WeChat: "Mary." Apparently, Mary was a cryptocurrency investor in Shanghai. I reached out to her and she agreed to meet. I was totally unable to glean any info about who she was from the exchange. I initially assumed she didn't speak English, as all her responses were one word and failed to really address my questions. Still, I convinced my dad that we needed to make a side trip to Shanghai before returning to the States.

Even though I didn't really know who she was, I wanted to put on a good face. Preparing to meet her in my hotel restaurant for afternoon tea, I dressed up in my brand-new Taiwanese tailored suit. She was waiting for me in a dirty t-shirt and loose jeans. I felt a bit silly, but hyper-casualwear isn't unusual in tech so I didn't have much of an opinion. When we got to talking, 17-year-old me was blown away. She told me she was an early investor in Alibaba, an even earlier investor in Bitcoin, and used to work in hedge funds on Wall Street. And here she is talking to me, a yet-to-graduate high school schmuck.

She was pretty easygoing at first, so I acted on what I presumed to be the biggest opportunity of my life and began explaining my business plan. I barely got into it before she told me it was a horrible idea, that I was an idiot, maybe the biggest in the world, and didn't understand anything. Seriously, how could I possibly think that was a good idea? She absolutely ripped into me for a solid 15 minutes, not allowing me to get in a single word. Then she offered me a job.

Chapter 2

Getting the Job – Moving to Shanghai

"Of course, being a body builder, coding is strictly performed in gym shirts and no shirt. Or a luxurious (open) bathrobe."

My first time stepping off the plane in China at 15 years old was addictive. All of my senses suddenly, almost violently, forced to recalibrate to completely foreign sensations. Now, just two years later, I was sitting at the Ritz-Carlton Pudong in Shanghai, wearing my sport coat and getting absolutely destroyed by my new investor contact. The berating ended only with the challenge that if I wanted a chance of having a clue, I'd have to move to Shanghai and work for her.

    I was confused by the job offer coming on the tail end of a 15-minute rant about my idiocy. The complete lack of details about the nature of the job only added to my confusion. *Move to Shanghai and work for me* was all the clarity I was going to get. But she was serious, and I was not going to refuse the opportunity, whatever it was.

She told me we'd work the logistics out over WeChat in the following weeks. In the meantime, I went back to America to graduate high school. My partner and I had received some press for our project, so he and I briefly went to New York and met with the "biggest" company in the cryptocurrency space, and talked generally about being absorbed into them. At that time, they were known for bringing all the best projects built on Ethereum on board. It would have been massive for our potential to raise money, but the talks went nowhere.

I also went to college orientation, as at this point I still planned on attending. But orientation made me resolute that I would never go to college if I could figure out anything else to do. I already hated school, and this three-day snapshot shattered any illusion I had that the hatred had abated. It became apparent to me that the only difference between high school and college was going to be a bigger bill and a shittier living arrangement. My focus was trained on my offer in Shanghai.

But the offer still lacked clarity. Mary wouldn't communicate much on WeChat, and even when I finally got her on the phone, it led to more questions than answers. I didn't know the scope of the work, whether or not I'd be compensated, or where I'd live. She promised to provide housing, but there were no details on location or type of accommodation. I had no contract, no visa sponsorship, no details on living arrangements, just an invitation to show up on a tourist visa.

When Mary and I had met in Shanghai, I tried to ask about the work she and her company were doing but only got vague answers. At the time, I was embarrassed, as if I had just failed to understand what she was talking about. But really, she was just rambling. It wasn't until after I got to the States that she finally sent the name of her main project. I Googled it. Hard to find, the main website was buried, and the site itself was a sparse html page with links to the coin's wallet and some scientific papers describing how it worked. I couldn't make sense of them.

The only other info I could find online was an "AMA" or "Ask Me Anything" event the anonymous founder had done in a chatroom. I couldn't believe what I was reading. The response to a throwaway "Who are you?" question dove into the darknet, anonymous coders with security clearances, and Russians:

> **I am not sure I have seen anything about who you are? What is the dev team size? Background?**
>
> *I think there are over ~60 people who have worked on [project] or have made major contributions. It's really a project from the darknet. Many of the contributors are anonymous. Some of them have security clearances and were in the military industrial complex... We also have a lot of very very early Bitcoin people, hardcore crypto people that predate Bitcoin and an Ethereum core developer, etc. ... Then we have people who are a part of Israeli and US intelligence... this group seems very interested in the*

Getting the Job – Moving to Shanghai

> 'applications' of these coins. … Then a lot of people from the deep darknet, anon, frog twitter and cypher punks and bitorrent communities. And people from the Russian darknet community. We have like eight Ivans.

The AMA and my confusing interactions with Mary were all I had to work with in my attempt to understand what I was getting myself into.

These unknowns were annoying, but not dealbreakers. I wanted this to happen. I figured worst-case scenario, I got there, found out it was all air, and left, either back to the US or elsewhere in Asia. The only thing that made me slightly nervous was when Mary finally sent me my address in Shanghai, a couple of days ahead of my planned arrival. I checked the map. It was an hour outside of town in what seemed to be an industrial area on the outer ring called Baoshan. Whatever. If it's too bad I'll just pull the ripcord.

I got to Shanghai on July 1st, 2017. For the first two days I stayed in a hotel. At some point I met with a local venture capital group to pitch my original business idea. Again, I was told that I was stupid. On the third day I ventured out of town to see my new pad. The area was a bit rundown but not horrible or empty. I still didn't really speak Chinese at this point, but I was the only foreigner coming into that building anyway, and they were expecting me. They had a room card waiting for me with "American" written on it in Chinese. The lobby decorations were sparse aside from a sign with the name of the complex and a poster that said, "This community is united by strong anti-Japanese sentiment."

They took me up to my new apartment —a small room with no windows. The bed was a wooden plank on the tile floor. The bathroom was a small shower with a toilet in it. There was a wardrobe, a sink, a small refrigerator and a desk. I started laughing, but it wasn't going to be that funny to me for long. I went back out and bought a comforter for my wooden bed. That night I felt the weight of my decision, alone in China, in that room, sitting on my plank.

Luckily, I wasn't given much time to sit and sulk. The next morning, I went to "work" for the first time. Mary's office was just down the street from my room in a complex built by the government for tech start-ups. It held the hope of likeminded people working near each other with a common goal. But also had the sort of emptiness of a government-engineered community on the far outskirts of town that attracted groups that could not afford to actually pay any rent.

I strode into the office ready to start my new life, but Mary wasn't there.

I was informed by her assistant that she wasn't in China at the time and wouldn't be back for about a month. I asked if she'd mentioned any plans or instructions for me. None. But the assistant said she'd check with the guy running one of Mary's projects to see if he wanted my help. Just my luck, he wanted an intern. I took a seat and waited.

Eight hours later, just as I was getting ready to give up on Mary and Shanghai, he showed.

After the initial handshake and introduction to my new boss, Michael, my first impression was that he was totally stimmed out. He probably was. Disheveled, constantly fidgeting, mind and speech going a million miles a minute only to be interrupted by sudden, hysterical laughter.

I assumed we'd stay at the office and talk about his project, but he immediately commanded me to follow him out to the street where we waited for a car. A brief interview ensued: He asked me what my major was. I didn't want to say I had only just graduated high school, so I picked what I hoped would sound the best to him and said "math". Good call. He nodded and praised, *good, good, yes, math is good.* He only stopped saying *good* because the driver called him, at which point he immediately handed the phone to me asking, *you speak Chinese, right?* At that point, no, not really, but I still managed to guide the driver to our location in extremely mangled Chinese. We got in the car and headed off.

Here I am with no idea where we're going, in the back of a car with a guy I just met five minutes ago who seemed to be on speed. But as I started prodding him about the crypto market, I could immediately tell he was a genius. In the 20-minute car ride he covered more knowledge on all aspects of crypto and finance than I had ever heard. But our conversation was cut short, and I was reminded of the reality of my situation when we arrived at a residential compound. Looking back on it I feel it was probably unnecessary paranoia, but at the time I was very on edge. The compound was pretty run down, in what I now understand to be typical Chinese fashion — gardens, ponds, and recreation areas designed to be extravagant when the compound was built, only to have no one maintain them whatsoever within a few months of opening. As we got in the elevator up to the top floor of one of the buildings, I had no idea what to expect.

We entered his apartment and it was straight out of a movie. I hate saying that — really, I think people try way too hard to feel like "my life's a movie bro" — but this *did* feel like a movie.

Contrary to my expectation of a small, rundown apartment, it was very nice and surprisingly big. Two floors. The first floor had a huge living room that had been turned into a hacker den. Cords everywhere, multiple workstations with three to four monitors each, research files all over the place, big whiteboard scribbled with tech plans. Wall-to-wall, floor-to-ceiling shelves filled with all the supplements and nootropics that exist. Robot prototypes and experiments strewn around. Lots of empty coconuts shells (I guess they need the electrolytes for their huge brains).

Michael told me which computer was to be mine and listed about 100 tasks in 15 seconds. I asked him to repeat himself. He told me I needed to get better short-term memory.

At this point it was already around 8 p.m. and I figured he assumed I'd be working through the night. I jotted down all I could remember of what he said and got to work. It was actually not so complicated, basically amounting to setting up new computer systems for the room. Eventually, the door opened and a body builder walked in. This body builder turned out to be second in command of the project, James. We shook hands. Michael told him I was sent by Mary, and then his first words to me were, *Are you a diplomat's kid or something?*

What had I gotten myself into?

Talking to James in person was like talking to Mary over WeChat. Brief, light on detail, but at least James got to the point. Maybe a total of 10 words an hour. Most of his time he spent laser focused on his coding, and most of his breathing was done through a massive vape. Of course, being a body builder, coding is strictly performed in gym shorts and no shirt. Or a luxurious (open) bathrobe.

I don't remember how late I stayed that first night. I worked for a while and also spent some time talking to Michael. Eager to understand his background in cryptocurrency and life, I asked about his path and what led him to China. He said he'd previously been living in California but became convinced the US government was going to start assassinating or disappearing all the early Bitcoin contributors, such as himself. He didn't want to be murdered in a no-knock raid and figured China was the best place to avoid such a thing. He made the move to Shanghai and quickly established himself in local networks via Mary.

I realized that night this was exactly my place, my people. Sincerely. After a lifetime of being forced to waste my time in school, I was finally free and in my ideal environment. In school I was surrounded by people who didn't want to be there (myself included) working on things that meant nothing. Now I was with two no-nonsense, serious guys *who wanted to be there*, and who were deeply committed to and knowledgeable about their work.

I wanted to really prove my worth and earn a permanent place on their team. Even though the crypto market hadn't even started going crazy yet, I felt huge potential in being with these guys.

Chapter 3

Crypto Primer

"It didn't matter what you did in this market. As long as you took action and took it fast, you'd make money."

What was happening in 2017 that allowed 17-year-old me to find myself in this situation in the first place? It basically all boils down to this: loads of money were being poured into the cryptocurrency market, and people were becoming — or expecting to become — rich overnight by investing.

The mainstream timeline officially begins in 2009 with the release of Bitcoin. In the mass consciousness, this was the first cryptocurrency. In reality, it had predecessors, but they are long since irrelevant. Bitcoin is a digital currency with no central issuer or authority. You hold it in a digital wallet on your computer, and if you want to send it to somebody, it is sent peer-to-peer, directly between wallets, with no intermediary. When you send a wire transfer between banks, it takes days and can have heavy fees — especially if wiring internationally — as each bank involved has various accounting and regulatory compliance measures to tend to. Not to mention they simply work at a slow pace. Sending Bitcoin between computers takes minutes and has a miniscule fee, making no distinction between you sending money to your neighbor or to China.

To ensure transactions are secure and legitimate, Bitcoin transactions over the internet aren't simply handled by the sender's computer and the recipient's computer, but by a network of computers all running the Bitcoin software. Instead of a central bank keeping a ledger, a network of thousands upon thousands of computers (called "miners") verify each and every transaction. If you attempt to make a transaction that doesn't adhere to the protocol, say, spend more Bitcoin than you really have, it will be rejected by the network. Every fulfilled transaction has been verified by this network and recorded into an immutable, publicly available ledger shared by each computer in the network. This ledger is what's referred to as the "blockchain", Bitcoin's underlying technology.

Bitcoin is an ideological project at its core, which quickly gained a cult following of internet libertarians, anarchists, hackers, etc. acting in response to the global financial crisis of 2008. They rejected the global financial order, and primarily the idea of fiat currency that can be printed at the whim of a central bank. Bitcoin has a finite supply that cannot be changed. Bitcoin's early community wanted, in their words, a currency governed by *math*, not by *men*. They don't want to have to trust a central bank to do no evil when they can hard-code a digital currency to be innately incapable of doing evil, so to speak.

Bitcoin gained attention quickly, but not for good reasons. It had become the method of payment for an online drug marketplace called the Silk Road. Want to buy LSD online and have it shipped to your doorstep? Use Bitcoin. It was infamous for being the currency of choice for criminals worldwide.

It also gained notoriety for its volatility. Bitcoin, worth less than a penny upon conception in 2009, by late September 2013 it was valued over $120, and then rallied to over $1,000 by December. Critics and evangelists were equally excited by this. The critics could point to the volatility as a sign of the project being totally non-viable as a legitimate currency. The evangelists who held from a penny, now rich, weren't as concerned with these logistics. The party was cut short, however, when an exchange was hacked. Bitcoin's price plummeted back down to around $200 and continued to trade more or less sideways for quite some time.

The cryptocurrency world was fairly quiet for a period after the 2013/14 action. There were other serious currencies on the scene now, such as Litecoin, but no currency maintained the following Bitcoin did, and even Bitcoin's following was fairly small at that point. But things began to change after a new project, Ethereum, was released in 2015.

Ethereum took the concept of Bitcoin — distributed execution of transaction accounting — and applied it to computer applications. Ethereum is, simply, a distributed computer. You write programs on Ethereum like you'd write any other computer program, then the execution of said program is run and validated on a distributed network, like Bitcoin. This quickly became popular because you could very easily create your own cryptocurrency. Of course, you could do that before, but you needed a following to comprise the distributed network. With everyone building a coin on Ethereum, the Ethereum network itself grew significantly, and everyone could piggyback off of that.

It was late-2016 when I got involved in cryptocurrency. Ethereum had been out for a while and was gaining popularity from people making new coins on top of it. The overall cryptocurrency community was growing faster than ever before, largely around excitement over the advent of the "Initial Coin Offering", or ICO. New Ethereum-based projects were popping up daily, often just re-hashing typical internet businesses like VPNs, but this time there was a digital currency attached. Because Ethereum made it so easy, these new projects would develop a coin and a nice website explaining their business idea, then sell the coin in an ICO to raise money for the production of the promises on the website. The vast majority of these never came to fruition — after they'd already raised the money, of course.

While the ICOs were more or less always of dubious quality, I have to say that the people who comprised the cryptocurrency space at this time were great to work with. December 2016, I'm coming into the market as a nobody 17-year-old with an idea and a lot of spare time. Yet I could easily talk to, and get offers of assistance from, those running the biggest projects. Within a few weeks, I was invited to talk about my idea on a podcast. Everyone was in the same chatrooms, the same internet forums, collaborating and trying new things. Trying to push the limits of the technology. The business/marketing types were nearly non-existent. It was just a bunch of deep hobbyists — really smart people, some too smart for their own good, having a good time and working on things that interested them.

The ICOs were getting bigger and bigger, though, and caught the attention of the get-rich-quick types. With each passing day the number of scammers and non-technical people increased exponentially. There was no regulatory framework for any of this and it was truly, to repeat the trope, the "Wild West". ICOs for software that didn't exist started raising tens of millions of dollars with ease, pumping their own coin price and the price of Bitcoin and Ethereum alongside it, as the excitement growing around cryptocurrency increased.

This was the environment that allowed for a 17-year-old recent high school graduate to be hired by a Chinese angel investor and move to China on a whim. A combination of genuine hobbyist's spirit for open collaboration, a pragmatic belief that I could make her money, and a sense of urgency. It didn't matter what you did in this market. As long as you took action and took it fast, you'd make money.

Chapter 4

First Taste of Things to Come

"James could rightfully point out that I had no value to the project, but it's hard to dent the ego of a 17-year-old who is flying from Shanghai to Taipei just to party for a few nights."

I worked hard that first month. It was 115 degrees outside every day that summer, and every morning I left at 7 and either went to a coffee shop or Michael's apartment to work, then went home to sleep around midnight. It helped that my apartment was a dump and I couldn't stand being in it.

    I was getting to know as much about the project, and how I could earn my place, as possible. The tasks Michael gave me were many, but manageable, coding up dumb little tools like Twitter price-ticker bots as a test of my ability. I honestly didn't know how to do 90% of the coding, but given a task I'd disappear to a coffee shop and teach myself. Michael frankly seemed more concerned in gauging my loyalty than testing my coding ability. Every morning he would hand me a random handful of assorted pills and then watch to see if I would take them. If they weren't out of sight within a couple minutes, he'd start yelling. *What are you waiting for?* I knew the pills weren't drugs per se, but rather nootropics/supplements, so down the hatch they went.

A few weeks in, I took a solo weekend trip to Beijing to meet up with online crypto people and got taken out to dinner by some guys from Bitmain, the biggest producer of Bitcoin mining hardware. Peking duck and discussion of the market. Lots of people didn't like Bitmain and felt they exercised too much control over what was supposed to be a decentralized system. They told me this was a baseless claim. They impressed upon me that it was important that they control the system so they can ensure it's decentralized. Oh, I see. First business dinner of my new life in China. Good time.

As I mentioned before, the crypto market hadn't taken off yet like it would later that fall and winter. However, our project was well funded, and I got an early taste of the big spending to come. I came to China with $2,000 that I had accumulated over 17 years of life, and was penny pinching hard in my daily spending. One day, Michael told me he'd pay me a bit if I built a small tool for our crypto's wallet application. It was a few hours' worth of work. I told him I'd get right on it; he sent me $4,000.

This task, and my general acclimation to their lifestyle in Shanghai gave me a nice first taste of what the bubble would bring. I spent almost all day every day with them, dining at different places across town every night, going out drinking, staying in drinking, staying in vaping and drinking. They covered the tab for me everywhere. It was a lot of fun. Work hard/play hard kind of thing.

At the end of the month I wanted to take a week off to go to Taipei and meet friends for my birthday. But I was starting to feel like I had responsibilities for the first time, and the company was getting busier and busier. I was afraid of being seen as absentee in these potentially crucial moments. I asked James what he thought and he said to go, I was still useless right now anyway. Fair enough.

James could rightfully point out that I had no value to the project, but it's hard to dent the ego of a 17-year-old who is flying from Shanghai to Taipei just to party for a few nights. I felt huge. Two months removed from high school, it felt cool to say that I was blowing out of Shanghai to celebrate my birthday in Taipei.

Early August and the time was coming for a decision as to whether I'd go back to the US for college or stay in China. I had no offer of full-time employment, so I went to see Mary, who had finally reappeared in Shanghai. I asked her to formally hire me and she turned me down. Without a college degree, she couldn't get me a work visa, and she didn't have any full-time work for me, anyway. I was crushed until I remembered this was the first time I had seen her all summer, and the real authority in the project should lie with Michael. But he wouldn't give me any guarantee either. He didn't turn me down, he just said things were slow and informal. If he had work and I was around, he'd give it to me.

This wasn't enough to run with, at least not immediately. I called my parents for input; they said it was my decision, and a hard one at that.

I remember one long night in particular, leaving Michael's after failing to get any guarantee of employment. I paced back and forth for hours on the sidewalk down the street from his place, drinking through the gallon jug of water I was carrying around, and debating what to do in my head as I watched hookers come and go from the secret backdoor entrance to the brothel across the street.

Eventually I went home, went to sleep, and woke up with the conclusion that I had to give it a shot. If it failed, I would just go back to school in the winter. As long as business picked up for the project, I'd have work to do.

Chapter 5

Finally, Gaining Momentum

"He promised me $10,000 if I'd stay up for three days straight helping him get it done. Deal."

Business, however, didn't pick up. In fact, in August and September I basically did nothing but sit around watching YouTube all day. I got a new apartment in the hip part of downtown — the Former French Concession. A sort of mini-Europe in China. The apartment had windows and a bed, which was nice, but I was bored out of my mind and beginning to expect I'd have to accept college soon.

    The business technically wasn't dead, just really, really slow. People came to town every few weeks to meet Michael, and he'd take me along on the meetings. My role slowly started shifting from being just another programmer to being his personal assistant. That was the only thing that really needed doing anyway, at least until the first sign of the bubble came in mid-October.

Finally, Gaining Momentum

A guy running some Bitcoin spinoff called Michael in a panic. He wanted to cash in on the "Initial Coin Offering" (ICO) craze. Initial Coin Offerings were how crypto millionaires were being minted. At that time, while crypto prices weren't going up that much, people were still able to raise tens of millions of dollars by putting together a nice website with a whitepaper that described their new theoretical coin, and then going public.

The guy on the phone with Michael was panicked because he had his ICO scheduled to start in three days but he hadn't actually produced a coin or hired any programmers. Michael was promised $500,000 if he could get everything made in time for the ICO. He promised me $10,000 if I'd stay up for three days straight helping him get it done. Deal.

I didn't leave his house for three days as we tried to get the project done as quickly (and cheaply) as possible. Michael didn't want to code it himself, but instead hired the cheapest Indians he could find on the internet to throw it together. My job was to coordinate tasks between the various coders and report any problems to Michael. The problem with this strategy was that while it was very, very cheap… there's a reason for that. What they built didn't work at all, partly because they were all siloed apart from each other in their tasks, with just me passing info between them, and partly because none of them were competent programmers to begin with.

We didn't deliver a working codebase in time. I stayed up for three days straight, non-stop messaging developers and fixing payment issues with the recruiting website to no avail. I didn't get my $10,000.

On the flipside, the episode solidified my place in Michael's view as his "executive assistant." James still didn't see much use for me, but we got along well personally and he ended up moving into my new apartment since he was sick of listening to Michael talk while he tried to code. With my position established, I just needed to add to it on my own initiative. Recalling how I had historically presented my own project at various meetups, along with hearing Michael and James complaining about a lack of marketing, I pitched a new idea to them. I'd travel to various major Asian cities and act as the project's spokesperson, presenting at large meetups and conferences. Neither Michael nor James really enjoyed dealing with people, so the idea was accepted. I began reaching out to different clubs, conferences, and meetup groups, and was invited to speak in Tokyo.

I put together a presentation and a plan for a two-day trip. Michael approved and sent me the money that I'd requested. It was only a two-and-a-half-hour flight, so I flew roundtrip coach and applied the money saved on airfare toward a luxury hotel.

The first business trip just felt *right*. I always enjoyed traveling with my family, especially in Asia, and now I had a job where I could frequently travel in luxury throughout Asia on someone else's dime. It was a dream. Yes, the clock was stopped there — five months and eight days after graduating high school I officially realized my dream job.

Finally, Gaining Momentum

I'd been to Tokyo once before, but it was only for three nights and I wasn't familiar with the city. I asked a local friend that I'd met a few months earlier in Shanghai to take me around to fulfill my typical routine in a foreign city: get coffee, eat, walk walk walk, get coffee, eat, get a drink or two, walk walk walk, call it a day. I take in the experience of new cities by walking aimlessly for hours on end, fueled by occasional coffee and food breaks. First day in Tokyo was enjoyed as such. Second day more or less the same, then I spent some time in the afternoon preparing for my presentation. It wasn't expected to be a huge crowd, maybe 50 people in attendance.

I'm not naturally a social butterfly, but I realized that if I was going to become the project spokesman, the situation demanded I become one. I forced myself to assume the role. The key in this kind of situation, whether it's walking into a conference and trying to accumulate business contacts or walking into a club and trying to accumulate hot chicks, is to open the first person you see. Doesn't matter who it is. If you walk into a conference and the first person in your line of sight is a janitor you start talking to them. Gets the blood flowing.

The first person in my line of sight wasn't a janitor, though, it was a group of guys talking about something something Bitcoin. I immediately introduced myself, nervous and self-conscious about being only 18. Eventually I'd get over that when the bubble was in full swing and I was deep in delusions of grandeur. No one seemed to notice or care, though, that I was a teenager, and were happy to get to know me and discuss everyone's projects.

Deferred Admission

The crypto market in 2017 was comprised of two types of people: Genuine, hyper-dedicated hobbyists, and scammers. So there was no reason to be nervous as to whether or not people would care about my age. Among the hobbyists there was a strong openness and desire for collaboration. They couldn't care less about age (not to mention they were usually in the 18-25 range themselves). As for the scammers, why would they care about age? They were just trying to steal from you, and in this world a lot of the younger people had all the money.

By that point there was also a third group of people who had joined the crypto market — newcomers who had failed in other, more traditional professions and wanted to try and stake a claim in this new frontier. The Tokyo meetup was mainly comprised of this type, as well as some scammers. My presentation was solid, I presented it confidently, and it was very well received. Big win for my project and my personal role within it. Since most of the crowd were new to this market and I had the most technical, least sales-pitchy presentation, the entire crowd wanted to talk to me for insight at the end. After all, the host had introduced me as a cryptocurrency expert. It felt funny but I handled it well. Made some good contacts in Tokyo that I'd put to use again later.

After the presentation I tried to get a group of people to go out and party with me but I made the mistake of asking a group of foreigners instead of locals, and none of them wanted to since it was a work night. Eventually one woman agreed to a drink. But since Tokyo is the only place where white people still have to abide by drinking age rules in Asia, I couldn't even get into bars. She took me to an izakaya and ordered me a non-alcoholic beer, then pointed me to the wrong subway line, went home, and left me to figure out the rest of my night. Thanks.

I got a cab to Roppongi, a party district, and walked the streets getting endlessly harassed by Nigerians trying to lure me into dodgy clubs, then decided to call it a night and went back to my hotel. Flew out the next morning. First business trip and it was a massive success. At least the business part of it. I'd have to refine the partying aspect in later trips.

Chapter 6

Taiwanese Supermodels Sell Internet Scam Money

"Endless ideation, endless scams. The word 'disrupt' and phrases like 'paradigm shift', wielded like hammers and smashed into your skull over and over."

The opportunity to refine the art of the business trip appeared within a week of getting back to Shanghai. A small Ethereum conference was being planned in Taipei. Plus, the main crypto meetup group in Seoul finally got back to me with dates for a presentation. Here I made the rookie mistake of assuming the project was on a tight budget and offered to pay for the Taipei trip myself. Unnecessary and naïve, but ultimately inconsequential. I booked an itinerary for a day and a half in Taipei, two days in Seoul, then back to Shanghai.

The Taipei conference was the unofficial official starting bell of peak crypto insanity. The conference itself was a bore, even though the lineup of speakers was about as high-level as you could get. The founder of Ethereum, Vitalik Buterin, and other key Ethereum Foundation developers were present. Most of the attendees were local college kids — computer science students, a huge number of which had become Ethereum evangelists in the last year. Even though I was as much of an "insider" as you could be in that setting, I felt like an outsider and couldn't really click with those around me. Where others were excited about the talks, I could barely stay focused. Technical topics presented dryly by stereotypical computer nerds. Plus, there was a whacko twist where, for some reason, whenever the Ethereum crowd gets together like that, the nerds end up singing "Call Me Maybe" while donning unicorn t-shirts. I never really got it.

During a break between talks, a guy I hadn't met yet approached me and introduced himself. He was running a consulting business and his company was putting on an after-party that night. They'd rented one of the hot bars right across the street from the Taipei 101. Let me know he hoped I'd be able to make it. I appreciated that.

The party was set to start at 8, I got there just after. The bar was notably packed with something that had been missing from the conference — Taiwanese supermodels. There was also something notably missing from the bar that was in ample supply at the conference — nerds. Maybe my consultant buddy forgot to give them the invite.

Following my rule for accumulating contacts, I immediately opened the first two models on the bar. I had been talking to new people all day, so I was actually already in massive confidence/social butterfly mode. I was well received. They spoke perfect English, which made the conversation smooth since I still didn't speak great Chinese. Besides, the high-class 'hot' Taiwanese women in the bars and clubs around the 101 take such pride in being international, with their perfect California English, that they refuse to speak to you in their native language even if you speak it fluently.

    The nice girls let me know all the models had been hired for the night by a company that made a new coin for paying live streamers. The party wasn't just a party, it was an ICO pitch contest, and one of the pitching companies had brought in all the models to distract partygoers from actually listening to the pitch and realizing it was a scam. I still have some video from the pitch. *So we are basically like the Google Play of... like the Uber of...* yeah, whatever. Protip: If someone is pitching their business to you and at any point draws comparison to Uber/Airbnb/Netflix, or says what a "disruptor" they're going to be, walk away immediately.

    The models were whisked away from me by their manager; they had to go look good elsewhere. I turned my attention to accumulating business contacts. I saw some guys I'd met when I presented in Taipei earlier that year, so I went and had a drink with them. They introduced me to more and more people, each new person and their accompanying new business idea all increasingly showing signs of the impending bubble.

We're making a Bitcoin movie…

We're the Airbnb of…

We're going to disrupt Uber from disrupting…

Endless ideation, endless scams. The word "disrupt" and phrases like "paradigm shift", wielded like hammers and smashed into your skull over and over and over until you talk like that, too. In their defense, many scams don't know they are scams. They're just in over their heads. Idealists confused as to why they're receiving weird looks when explaining to potential customers that they expect to release the first minimum viable product in over a decade. I did also meet some solid people that night. The guys running the party, even if "consulting" is questionable, clearly knew how to throw a party, which is a useful marketing tool. There was also a Taiwanese legislator there, which surprised me, but we had a drink and I learned that he was leading a push for building a regulatory sandbox for cryptocurrency businesses in Taiwan. They wanted to be "Crypto Island", a term that other partygoers would eventually co-opt and ruin.

All in all, Taiwan was an even bigger success than Tokyo had been, even though I did almost no direct promotion of our project. I garnered government, business, and media contacts at the party that I made excellent use of going forward.

The Seoul trip was not so successful. It was the worst of my first three business trips.

Deferred Admission

First of all, it was very cold, which I was not prepared for, and I felt sick. Then I gave the exact same speech that I presented in Tokyo and found that what had been a smash hit for an audience of uninitiated rubes did not play the same for an audience of serious programmers. They grilled me on all the technical aspects of the project, which I was simply not prepared for. I looked like a fool or a scammer. I had also arranged through a friend from Taipei to have his friend, a local Korean, take me out drinking. We met for coffee and he said to call him when my presentation was done and he'd show me a great night out. I got a message after the presentation from his friend saying he broke his phone, couldn't meet me that night. Never heard from him again. I went to the party district on my own, couldn't work up the enthusasm to really go out, got a slice of pizza, and left. Flew back to Shanghai the next morning.

The failure of the Seoul trip didn't really bother me since Taipei was such a massive success. I was batting 2 for 3 so far and that was good enough. My position in the project was perfect and now we were heading straight into the massive market frenzy.

Chapter 7

Road Trip

"I had officially forgotten that I was a teenager, so I didn't feel out of line at all berating this guy."

The bubble was in full swing in December 2017. ICOs were still massively popular and raising increasingly disgusting amounts of money. Bitcoin was trading towards $20,000, ten times higher than the mark it hovered around when I got to China in July. Everyone who didn't already have a piece of the pie was scrambling to get involved, and Michael, partly through his own promotion and partly through promotion by Mary, had become a sort of go-to guy globally for people looking to make a new coin.

People were flying in from all over the world on what felt like a daily basis to meet with us. But Michael was too busy to really help all these people. His main focus was getting his own project ready to benefit from the bubble. So everyone who wanted him ended up being directed to me. People flew in from

France, Israel, the States, or wherever to meet with Michael and would end up discussing their business plan over lunch with me. Michael told anyone who contacted him to call me, I was head of his new coin business. But that didn't really exist, so I had to wing it. I reasoned that my (failed) experience juggling Indian programmers in October was sufficient.

Obviously, I'm not a person who feels that a lack of credentials or formal experience is a valid reason I can't do something. It's really not. I took the task seriously and handled this flood of new business perfectly. I dealt with bankers, mining executives, solar power investors, everything you could imagine. Everyone wanted a coin.

My first assignment was a group of Russians based in Shanghai who wanted help marketing their new coin. One night they called to set up an introductory meeting. Sent me a street location. I walked over. Waiting for me on the street was this guy, Roman, who I'd briefly met before. He told me to come with him and walked me down an alley into a small shop they were using as an office. Inside were a few other Russian guys and a few girls — either models or normal Russian women, I can't tell the difference.

Growing up in the US gives you messed up ideas on a lot of things. For instance — Russians. I was on edge. Don't f*ck with these guys. Don't look at them funny. Stay sharp, these are the people I've been fighting the last few years in Call of Duty: Modern Warfare. Red Dawn. They offer me a cigarette. *You smoke?* Yeah, of course. Blending in perfectly. We end up going to a restaurant and talking about their project over dinner. I was surprised by two things: one, we drank no vodka. Two, these were normal people, just like you and me. Unbelievable. I thought Russians were a different species. They were all great guys. Even when you know everything you've been taught is a lie you can still get caught up in some of it.

The Russian's project had an odd journey. I'd say it fell into the category of "it's a scam, but they didn't know it." It was a far-fetched idea, like many ICOs at the time, but the founders were genuinely trying to make it work. Aside from Michael's input, they certainly had some interesting local connections, including a small-time Chinese TV star, but they never really gained any traction and the project, for whatever reason, just seemed to go wrong at every turn. I took a small consulting fee to connect them with people Michael probably would have given them for free and wished them well. At that point in the market, aggressively and shamelessly pitched ICOs were definitely capable of exploding higher, but these Russians, contrary to my Grand Theft Auto upbringing, just weren't interested in being aggressors.

Other than the Russians, almost every other referral came from Mary, who I hadn't talked to since she denied me a job offer in July. She didn't even know I was still in China. She spent all of her time traveling the world and attending conferences on every continent, collecting contacts and pitching her investments. Recently she'd started pitching her new coin production business to people, by which she meant Michael would build them a coin, which then meant Michael would redirect their inquiry to me.

Mary invited about 30 people from her global network — some already in business with her, some interested in doing business with her — to form a delegation and run a road trip throughout China to present her various projects, ours being one of them. A conference was organized at each stop on the trip — Shanghai, Xi'an, Nanning, and Guangzhou. The focus of the Shanghai conference was our project, the focus of the Xi'an and Guangzhou stops remained unclear to me, and the Nanning stop was to meet the backers of the new coin for a Burmese separatist region. Admittedly cooler than our project.

The first night after everyone had flown in, a banquet was held at a nearby restaurant. I didn't feel like going and neither did James, so I felt justified in my absence since he was second in command. Then Michael called and screamed at me over the phone to get there immediately. Bring James. Whoops.

We got there and I was introduced to everyone. Mary was surprised to see me. She had never been told that I had not left China, but she didn't seem to care that I didn't listen to her. Instead she told the group the story of how she discovered me and knew I was special from the moment she met me, knew she had to take me under her wing. It was a nice story, a nice introduction to the group. Not exactly how I remember it, though.

A supposed "market maker" had flown in from India on Michael's invitation and was eager to make a deal with us. I say "supposed" because at this point there were tons of people offering their services as market makers, increasing the volume and, ideally, the price of your coin across whatever crypto exchanges it may be listed on. Having good volume/liquidity on an exchange is critical for any coin — the layman needed to be able to read the market price and submit an order of any size based on that price without looking at the order book, bid-ask spread, etc., and have it be filled instantly and as expected. Otherwise it's simply too difficult, and difficult means people give up and don't buy, and if they don't buy the price never goes up. The problem here was that of the people soliciting their services as market makers, 99% of them were scammers. I didn't know this yet, though, and this was my first experience with one.

This guy in particular was super high pressure. He wouldn't stop pushing for Michael to verbally commit to his proposal. He wanted to be given the right to buy around $1,000,000 worth of our coin well below the market price, and also be paid some sum of Bitcoin, which he would use to make markets. This is an obvious scam in retrospect. If you have a coin trading at a dollar on the market and sell someone $1,000,000 worth of that coin at $0.50 ($500,000), he'll just sell it at a dollar and pocket a $500,000 earn. I mean, why wouldn't you? And then he gets to say he "made markets" for you. One side of the market, at least. I guess no one was thinking it through very clearly at the time.

At the banquet, the responsibility of making a deal with this guy suddenly fell on me. I think Michael found him too annoying and eventually pointed at me, saying, *it's up to him*. I tried to pawn him off to James, but James wouldn't engage, and he seemed to enjoy watching me get annoyed trying to deal with the guy. I sat there talking through his proposal, told him I understood the details and would need to take some time to think about it, and that I'd let him know our decision at the conference the next day. Apparently, that was not a satisfactory answer.

He talked my ear off with all sorts of crap about why I needed to say yes immediately.

> *I came all the way out from India.*
> *I thought this deal was good to go.*
> *I just want to get the coin making money for everyone ASAP, you know?*
> *If I can't get my people on this right now it'll be too late.*
> *It's such a good deal what more is there you need to think about?*

I snapped. In front of everyone I started yelling at him to chill the f*ck out and stop asking me. I'll give you an answer tomorrow. Do. Not. Ask. Me. Again.

He didn't ask again.

I had officially forgotten that I was a teenager, so I didn't feel out of line at all berating this guy. At the end of the night I told James I didn't trust the guy the way he was pushing. I didn't have an assessment of the deal itself; he'd have to look at it. Ultimately, we didn't make the deal.

The conference the following day was uneventful. Other than making sure Michael got there to give his speech, I didn't have much of a role. Just a week before the conference I found out, for the first time, that we actually had a Chinese marketing team, and they spoke about our project to the audience. As usual I was mainly running interference for Michael, talking to people on his behalf and dealing with more inquiries into our new coin business. Someone in the local press might ask Michael about the significance of our project, Michael would veer off into a monologue on shrimp aquaculture in Mozambique, and then both would look to me for a usable soundbite.

That night we flew out to Xi'an. James didn't come, and I may as well have not gone. My family was coming to visit, and I was to meet them in Beijing directly from Xi'an, cutting the road trip short. All I did in Xi'an was drink. I didn't even go to the conference, just the banquets. We landed at midnight, but I'd taken a nootropic that morning for 'focus', so I was wired. I went out, couldn't even feel the effect of alcohol, went to sleep at 6 a.m., and most definitely felt the hangover when I woke up.

The one interesting thing that came out of Xi'an was Michael's "Kitty Cash" idea. "Crypto Kitties" had just become massively popular on Ethereum, and Michael wanted to create a version for our project as a marketing stunt. It was just a video game concept with collectible digital cats, like digital baseball cards. The catch was that Ethereum had limited processing power. As a result, when Crypto Kitties became popular and everyone was trading at the same time, it crashed Ethereum like your computer crashes when too many applications are open at once. Every business that uses Ethereum shares the same computer, so to speak, and so you had what were supposed to be serious financial business operations ground to a halt over digital cat trading. With our software, this wouldn't be an issue. Michael saw the opportunity to showcase our technology and became fixated on the idea. We started gathering developers to make the game immediately, and had designers draw up concept art.

The *concepts* for these cats would eventually sell for over a Bitcoin each, when Bitcoin was around $10,000. Not a bad business. While still in Xi'an, though, it was the only thing Michael cared to talk about, and the potential for digital cat concepts to sell for five figures was not clear to anyone but him. German bankers who had flown in from Berlin to discuss massive solar energy projects with him heard every minute detail of the game — how you will have to feed the digital cats or they die. Scarcity, that's how we pump the value. The cats can kill each other. You'll have to clean their e-litterbox. Our guests were surprisingly patient.

After the conference in Xi'an I took the train to see my family in Beijing. It was the first time I'd seen my dad since I moved to China. At that point I'd made some money and had a real position in the company, so there was a lot for us to talk about. We went to a few other cities, including Nanjing, home to Shanghai for a stop, and then on to Taipei for Christmas.

One-by-one the whole family got the flu, so the first few days in Taipei were all spent in bed. One of those days I got an unexpected message from Michael: *The market's about to go crazy, I have to get this compensation out and give you way more of our coin.* Sure. I had to bug him a few times over the next couple days to get him to follow through on that. I was expecting him to send ten or fifteen thousand. On paper our coin had exploded in value, and I really had no idea what to expect. He sent eighty thousand. I was eighteen. It was a good month.

The last night in Taipei, my consulting buddies were having another party in the same bar from the November conference. Gladly went to say hello to everyone again. I met some new people, which incidentally got me into the cool kid's club, and I was invited to the after-after-party in a private lounge. Much of the new crypto wealth at that time was immediately used to party. Of the 100+ people at the original party, maybe 15 of us went to the private lounge, where I was definitely the smallest fish. Other than the two consultants who threw the original party, the legislator I'd previously met was there, as well as some Silicon Valley investment types and London bankers. I blended in perfectly. Seriously, no one even slightly questioned my presence. Why would they? I genuinely believe I belong in that room, so I do.

I stayed there drinking and talking with everyone until around 2 a.m. Flew back to Shanghai that morning at 7. As usual, Taipei was worth the visit.

Chapter 8

Decadence

"Michael and I started buying ourselves jewelry. James started buying $30 watermelons."

December 2017 had marked the first full month of peak crypto bubble. It started picking up rapidly in the beginning of the month, and the mania officially culminated when Bitcoin hit $20,000 on December 17th. This was obviously a huge deal for our project since all the funds were in Bitcoin. Michael himself supposedly had thousands of Bitcoin since he'd been involved in its development from the early days. When I was in Taipei over Christmas, Michael messaged me every night asking if I wanted to come for lobster. I told him, every night, that I was out of town. I knew we were about to get extravagant.

Once I was back in Shanghai, the decadence moved in hard and fast. Michael and I started buying ourselves jewelry. James started buying $30 watermelons. When I arrived in China the previous summer, I dressed decently: polo shirt and khakis

Decadence

more or less every day. Now I'm walking into meetings in some obscene mix of hip-hop fashion circa 2004 and the hottest streetwear picked up at boutiques in Taipei, Chengdu, and Beijing. Think XXL skateboarding t-shirt from up-and-coming local brands with cargo pants/loose jeans/basketball shorts. Big gold chain with a Jesus piece and a pinky ring. Told people I was investing in gold. Hit my target of an ounce total holdings.

As my fashion was hitting hyper speed, our public persona was exploding. Industry media outlets frequently invited us for filmed interviews, and Michael wanted me to do them with him. I started getting comfortable on camera. Ego boost.

We went out every night. A typical night in Shanghai, January 2018, looked something like this:

5:00 PM: Dinner with my girlfriend. Something simple, local. I wasn't even that hungry to begin with.

6:00 PM: As I'm heading home, I get a message from Michael. Business dinner, at X steak house/osteria/fancy restaurant. Come ASAP. Investors from _____ are here. I immediately make my way over.

6:30 PM: Arrive at the restaurant. Typically, just me, Michael and James with guests, or sometimes a hodgepodge of other team members too. Anywhere from five to twelve people. Steaks, steaks, lamb racks, oysters, wine, liquor, steaks.

8:30 PM: Michael gets the check, then he, James, and I leave. Michael suddenly decides he wants sushi. We look up a good place and get a cab. Order lots of sushi and sake. This is an excuse to discuss the business, but somehow we continue eating. Sushi is delicious, after all.

9:30 PM: Here's where the night can go a few ways. Maybe we go to a wine bar so we can get champagne and charcuterie and discuss business plans. Or maybe we go to an Italian restaurant for some pizza. Maybe we go to a hooker bar to play pool with Vietnamese women and listen to Filipino cover bands singing Journey. Regardless of what we pick, the consistent theme is: we're not done eating and drinking. Nonstop consumption.

12 AM: Get invited to another bar/club by some Chinese friends. Depends on the mood. Sometimes Michael says he wants to go to the club, then he yells at us when we take him because it's too loud and disorienting. Night over.

Some people will read the above and think to themselves, *what a yuppie*. The ultra-rich will surely think, *you call this extravagance?* I'm not trying to paint a picture of us as the coolest guys on the planet living the most extravagant life money can buy. I bought a few thousand dollars' worth of gold jewelry. Great. The point is I was not expecting to be living like this barely six months out of high school. And Michael and James, who grew up without a ton of money, suddenly found themselves with what seemed to

Decadence

be infinitely deep pockets. A taste for more refined extravagance takes more time to develop than we were given.

Our profligate spending was mirrored by an equally appalling amount of money being lost to scammers. By this point they were unavoidable. I mean, getting scammed was avoidable, but if you had any profile whatsoever in our industry you were going to be bombarded with scam attempts 24/7. The severity of the scams ran the gamut. I paid a Czech YouTuber $1,500 to post a video review of our project. He posted it, collected payment, and deleted it the next day. This was a low-severity scam.

One day on my way to Michael's apartment, a partner of ours in London called. He was frantic. We had been pushing advertising and marketing efforts on a lot of fronts, one of which was video advertisements for YouTube and TV. Because we felt we had more money than God, the company strategy (which I ran but didn't come up with) was to hire around ten different video production firms at once, give them all the same script, and see who made the best video. Most of them were trash. Michael said he learned this from Steve Jobs and called it "the Apple strategy". I rolled with it.

The reason our London friend was frantic was because a supposed "big shot" director he'd recommended to us, and who we'd already paid, turned out to be a scammer. And he was about to try to finagle more money out of us.

Do not let him get on the phone with Michael, he told me.

This really was important. Michael, genius that he truly is, was proving very susceptible to scams. He was too trusting of people and didn't seem to mind risking money if there was a *chance* of a positive outcome.

The director knew that the way to Michael was through me, so he called me first. We'd paid him around $20,000 in Bitcoin to produce the advertisement. It was clearly written in the contract that he'd be paid in Bitcoin, not dollars or pounds or anything else. He got on the phone and started yelling at me: *What am I supposed to do with this Bitcoin? I have no way to sell it. You need to give me $20,000 cash and I promise it'll be worth your while. I've got the shoot lined up in Italy...* endless. Worse than the Indian market maker. I told him to f*ck off. He knew the terms; he'd been paid exactly according to the contract. He tried to give me a sob story, we went back and forth for a bit, but I made it clear to him it wasn't happening. Make the video or give us our money back.

I got off the phone with him and called London. He apologized profusely for recommending this guy and said he'd make it up to us. I told him not to apologize, just don't send us scammers in the first place.

Then I made the mistake of relaying the story to Michael. He insisted on yelling at the scammer himself for trying to pull a stunt like that. I told him no, it's already taken care of. He yelled at me for being insubordinate. I let him have his phone call. Within 10 minutes, he'd wired the scammer an extra $20,000. *Who knows? There's still a chance we'll get a great video out of it*, he said.

With money flying around so freely I decided to try to get some of my high school friends in on the action. My friend

Decadence

Charlie, who had been my original crypto business partner in high school, was already working on his own business in New York. Most of my other friends were in college, happily, and did not want to drop out. I slowly convinced one friend, who wasn't in college, to come to Shanghai. I wasn't sure exactly what he'd do, but I wanted to get someone out here to share in the lifestyle. Those days if you stood within ten feet of Michael, your bank balance would increase.

    He agreed to give it a shot, but another month or so passed before he flew out. In the meantime, money was coming in so fast (even given how much was being spent or scammed) that we had to figure out new avenues of investment for it. Just sitting on the crypto seemed great at the time, but Michael was determined to make investments in new, non-tech businesses as a hedge. This became my new primary role.

Chapter 9

Michael's Now a Crypto Billionaire

Thanks to the ramp up in crypto prices, and the success of our own project, Michael is reputedly a crypto billionaire now.

That's it… that's the chapter.

Chapter 10

Chinese Billionaires Buy Me Lunch

"In true Chinese business fashion, our local friends ordered a lot of alcohol, and lunch devolved into a drinking contest."

Another night, another impulsive call from Michael. This time he told me to go to the airport immediately. We were booked on a flight to Fuzhou, further down the Chinese coastline, where he'd set up meetings for us to go look at investing in local factories and potentially building out an office there using government incentives. I packed a backpack and by 11 p.m. was checked into my room at the brand-new downtown Hilton. As per ritual for me, if I arrive at night in a new hotel anywhere in Asia, I try out the room service burger. I'm not sure why I do this, but I do. This one was not good. And oddly enough I then got into an argument with the hotel because they wanted me to pay for it myself in cash, not allowing me to charge it to the room. The back and forth over the phone with the front desk was tiresome.

Just charge it to the room, it's on the company card.

No, no, you have to pay personally, we can't charge company card for room service.

Just charge the room, I'm not paying for this burger.

Oh.

It's midnight… I'm in a city I had never heard of three hours ago… and our coin has ratcheted 10 times higher in value. Why am I having this argument?

Next morning I got up early, got a coffee, and waited for Michael to call me. Eventually I was directed to meet him in the hotel restaurant for breakfast. The guys we were meeting with were on their way. One, a local, in banking and the other an American financier. *By the way, they're both billionaires*, Michael let slip as they made their way from the door to our table. Michael himself was allegedly a crypto billionaire at this point, too, which made me the only non-billionaire at the table, schmuck that I am.

They were nice guys. Perhaps an understatement when talking about billionaires, but it really was the first thing that struck me given the typical media portrayal that billionaire equals Bond villain. They talked a bit about their businesses.

The local runs foreign investments for a bank. The bank tells him their objective to own X type of business overseas, he needs to find a good deal. So his brother goes, finds a good deal, buys said business, then turns around and sells it to his brother at the bank. Sounds about right.

The American had investments everywhere. Factories and restaurants here in Fuzhou. A video game production studio. Lent the Cambodian government money to build parking lots and was also beginning work to build a new casino in the booming Sihanoukville — the Las Vegas (or perhaps Macau) of Cambodia.

After talking for a bit, we went out and saw the city. It was pretty run down compared with most of the places I'd been in China. Xi'an wasn't totally dissimilar, but you forgave it because it was interspersed with truly ancient history. Not so in Fuzhou. The few blocks of "ancient town" were just a tourist attraction built in the last decade. Endless 30-story concrete apartment towers make up the entirety of Fuzhou, even downtown. Drab. The overcast sky and every single building a matching gray. Ironically, Fujian, the province of which Fuzhou is capital, is sister states with my home state of Oregon. I thought Oregon deserved better.

We drove out and toured some factory space, during which time we were plainly informed that in addition to the cost of labor in the city being very cheap to begin with, we could also get prison labor for next to nothing through their connections. Good to know.

From factory space we went to look at office space downtown. The city was having a boom and getting a lot of money directly from the national government. There were all sorts of programs and new incentives for opening an office there. But it's a pretty backwater place and it was unclear what the real opportunity was other than just cheap real estate.

We went to lunch at a fancy place serving local specialties. In true Chinese business fashion, our local friends ordered a lot of alcohol, and lunch devolved into a drinking contest. Michael didn't want to drink, which was considered very rude. I did not need to be pressured to step up and salvage the situation by drinking with billionaires. It turned out ok. They were happy I spoke Chinese.

When the lunch finished, I went to look at more factories, drunk. My attention to detail may have been lacking. I was very bored of looking at factories.

The next day we went to the American financier's company office and sat down to discuss the new projects Michael wanted to develop. Michael's focus was very erratic now compared to when I first met him. The scope of things that called for his attention had increased a thousand-fold, and it became a source of tension for anyone who had to work with him on a specific task. Trying to clearly define the various projects he had in his head in the meetings in Fuzhou proved difficult. In preparation I scribbled down all of the projects I could recall, tiered by 1) whether or not they were cryptocurrency-related and 2) whether or not I actually understood them.

The top of the list was standard and easily explainable. Cryptocurrency miners, hardware wallets, and Kitty Cash. The further I went down the list, the further I confused everyone listening.

Submarine drones. Agricultural robotics. Smuggling gold out of Tanzania and selling it in Malaysia. Mauritian prawn farms. Establishing a blockchain-based central bank for Burmese separatists. Eventually our local partner pulled me aside and urged me to try and get Michael to focus. I said I'd try, but it's much easier said than done.

We did get into lease negotiations for a massive office space while we were there. Michael decided he wanted to open a startup incubator. You let enterprising college kids set up computers on your desks and take 70% of their business in return. I was to be head of construction and renovation. Another new role. This one never materialized, though.

I left Fuzhou after two days of meetings to go to Xiamen. I had no business goal there, I just heard it was a pretty city and wanted to see it. Was not let down. Xiamen was very refreshing after being in Fuzhou, with its colonial architecture, hilly terrain, and immense, maze-like network of alleyways dotted with boutique coffee shops. I felt Xiamen redeemed Fujian province as a worthy sister-state to Oregon. I flew back to Shanghai two days later and not 24 hours passed before I was headed back to the airport.

Chapter 11

I Live in the Airport

"I can easily wake up in Shanghai and be at my favorite coffee shop in Taipei by 10 a.m."

Whether for fun or business, I was in at least two cities a week for the first half of 2018. Always in the airport. I know Hong Kong International Airport like the back of my hand. The 4:30 a.m. drive out to Shanghai Pudong International, as much a morning routine as coffee. Nearly every major city in Asia is three hours or less by plane from Shanghai, and by always getting the first flight out, I can be checked in to my hotel and ready for a full day in a new place by 10 a.m. Local late sleepers aren't even up yet.

    I'm comfortable with traveling anywhere, but I've got Shanghai-Taipei travel down to a perfect science. Get up at 5:30 a.m., head to Hongqiao (the Shanghai downtown airport) for my 7 a.m. flight. Terminal is empty this early. I can reliably go from stepping out of the cab to sitting at the gate in under 25 minutes. Barring delays, I arrive at Taipei Songshan (Taipei downtown airport) by 8:30 a.m. Hidden gem of an airport — always empty. I don't check bags, but even if I did, I'd be through immigration and baggage claim within 10 minutes. With this method I can easily wake up in Shanghai and be at my favorite coffee shop in Taipei for morning coffee by 10 a.m. — only an hour or so later than I'd have my first coffee on a normal day. Unbelievably smooth.

Serious business travelers may laugh at me for suggesting my average of around two flights a week is noteworthy, but relative to the average person (and especially a teenager), it was insane. It's even more ridiculous considering I have a fear of flying. I hate flying. I'm on the edge of a heart attack for 100% of take-offs and landings. At the same time, it had become so routine that I feel very at home and in my element whenever I'm in an airport or on a plane. It's second nature.

After returning from Fuzhou and Xiamen, the next day I flew to Guangzhou, where I spent a whole 30 hours before heading to Shenzhen. Not long after Shenzhen I think I flew to Taipei, again. Can't remember why.

Guangzhou and Shenzhen were fun trips. At least Guangzhou was. James and I went to oversee the Chinese marketing team's meetups in these two cities. James's friend owns a vape shop in Guangzhou, so we met up with him and his friends, then headed out to a driving range not far from downtown to drink and hit balls. Next day we held the meetup, had dinner, then drove to Shenzhen.

A lot of people say they love Shenzhen, but I don't see how that can be true. I think they love the idea of it. It's a horrible city. There's nothing remarkable about it. Shenzhen has no history, it's just endless glass office buildings and malls, all built in the last 15 years. To get from one place to another takes an hour minimum. What people like is the idea that it's brand new, high-tech, etc. Fine. But the actual experience of being there sucks.

Outside the meetup there really was nothing to do there. James left before me and went to Hong Kong. I stayed the afternoon for a cup of coffee then flew back to Shanghai.

Chapter 12

Trouble from the Valley

"I was not sensitive enough at the time to recognize what was clearly a developing train wreck."

Scamming was still rampant in February and I was trying to get it under control, but we had lots of other things to focus on too. We wanted to get our coin on a major exchange as quickly as possible so we could maximize our upside exposure to the bubble. It was still difficult for the layman to actually purchase our coin, which was a massive problem. Most didn't even get to the point of trying to buy it because they hadn't even heard of it. Our marketing was severely lacking. Michael decided we had to bring in help.

He had a friend in Silicon Valley who agreed to come and take over our marketing operation. Michael was super excited to have him on board. He said his friend, Thomas, was a massively successful serial entrepreneur in the Valley who'd raised tens of millions of dollars in venture capital money for multiple projects over the last few years. He also was excited to report that Thomas usually just used the VC funds to live a luxurious personal lifestyle until the company went bust, then would start a new one. Thus, "serial" entrepreneur. Michael found this hilarious and didn't sense anything bad would come of it since such behavior is the standard for success in the Valley. He's not really wrong, but nonetheless didn't seem to grasp that this had negative implications for bringing him into your own company.

Thomas didn't have any intention of moving to Shanghai, where the project was more or less officially based, but he flew out to meet the executive staff, if you could call it that, and work out the details of his new role and tasks. The first night we had our typical excessive meal at a wonderful Turkish restaurant to welcome the new team member. The whole Shanghai team was present. The second night we did the exact same thing again at a different restaurant. Warm welcome.

He seemed like the typical Silicon Valley type, which I didn't totally click with. Flamboyant and geeky, yet sharp and confident — he definitely knew what he wanted and was going to get it. He immediately got to work replacing Michael's entire marketing structure and all the people who had any role in it (myself included) with his own people in San Francisco. I initially insisted that I retain my role in coordinating the volunteer contributions of enthusiastic internet community members, bestowed upon me by James, but Thomas made sure that his people took control of that too.

Trouble from the Valley

The main things his team took over were attending conferences in North America and Europe, and online marketing. Online marketing's biggest tasks at the time were to create a new website and write a white paper. Like I said before, projects were raising a hundred million dollars on these two things alone. We actually had a white paper, in proper form, which is to say that it was truly scientific and academic. It wasn't just a marketing paper. But that was apparently a problem and we needed a flashier one written, so Thomas's team got on that.

Once the entire non-Chinese marketing apparatus was in his hands, he began making budget demands. If I remember correctly, Michael told me his personal salary was around $25,000 a month. Then he wanted an additional $100,000-plus per month for conferences.

I was not sensitive enough at the time to recognize what was clearly a developing train wreck. Michael's outlook was that in high levels of business, the most successful people are sociopaths, so having self-described scammers around was good if you could get them to work for you. Too bad the "getting them to work for you" part was not handled very competently. After Thomas left Shanghai, he began doing exactly what Michael should have anticipated.

With the massive budget, Thomas gladly reported back to Shanghai that he was sparing no expense in preparing after-parties for upcoming conferences. He hired the best strippers in San Francisco and booked a suite at the Ritz to get buddy-buddy with media and exchange contacts from local blockchain conferences. For weeks Michael gleefully shared the selfie of

Deferred Admission

Thomas and the strippers with everyone he ran into — *See, I told you this guy was good.*

Aside from the absurd budget, Thomas's people, who no one else had ever met, were in control of our website, social media outlets, and all forms of communication with Western business contacts and community members. His team's internal communication was switched to a separate platform than ours in Shanghai. They were uncooperative. His team became bigger and bigger every day as all his friends joined and got on the payroll. Remote work managing a chatroom for a few hours a day, $10,000 a month. Thomas himself also constantly upgraded his title, going from Western Marketing Director, to Chief Marketing Officer, to Chief Operations Officer.

Michael had me planning trips to Cambodia and Mauritius to scout new, non-crypto projects for him, so I became fairly far removed from all the marketing drama, especially since my original involvement was revoked by Thomas's people. But Michael was becoming increasingly displeased with their performance and behavior. The Chinese marketing team was envious of their budget and constantly complained of misuse of funds. James recognized the precarious situation created by outsiders controlling the company's social media accounts and was trying to get Michael to claw back control.

The situation began to implode at the end of February. Some tech magazine did a hit piece on our project, claiming to dissect the nature of our "scam" so readers could avoid us. The piece was based on an interview with Thomas, who claimed to be our COO. The validity of this claim, as in whether or not Michael approved it, is still unclear to me. Anyway, Thomas gave some sub-par answers to loaded questions and had several other quotes taken out of context. Either way, the result was a viral hit piece with our "COO".

Thomas wanted to take the lead and use his marketing team to respond to the piece, but Michael took this as the signal to move against Thomas. He suspected it was all a manufactured crisis, led by Thomas himself. That he knew Michael wanted to move against him, so he would prove his worth by fixing the situation. I think this may well be true, although no evidence really ever appeared for or against it.

Michael emailed the writer of the hit piece, against the advice of the team and some very unhappy investors, saying that Thomas not only wasn't COO, but was uninvolved in the project entirely, and was just a random scammer trying to make money by faking association with it. Regardless of whether the COO title was valid or not, Thomas's association with the project had been officially recognized for a while at this point, and the magazine had a field day with Michael's response. A new piece came out, titled something to the effect of, "We thought this project was a scam. Now we're *certain* it's a scam". The new article started with Michael's email, followed by exhibits A through Z of official project social media channels promoting Thomas's involvement in the project.

Obviously, this was the end of friendly relations between Thomas and Michael. Thomas claimed he was owed more money. Michael claimed he'd been conned. Both sides claimed they'd been slandered. Lots of talk about lawsuits, not sure any were ever filed.

It took a few months of drama, but eventually all project accounts were recovered and our friends from the Valley went away. Both sides had threatened a lot, but nothing really came of it. Rumors spread that James was really the one who brought Thomas in, and that Michael had been against it from Day One.

Honestly, whether or not they intentionally scammed the project is an unsettled question to me. I'm inclined to believe they did, just from the impression I got from my initial interactions with Thomas in Shanghai, as well as online interactions with his team later on. Or maybe his team was just annoying to work with and got away with a lot because they knew it would be permitted. Regardless, this must have been the most expensive "scam" we suffered up until that point, and certainly caused the most drama. Little did I know, it could get a lot worse. However, it would be almost half a year before that was revealed to me, and in the meantime, I had a lot more of the bubble left to enjoy.

Chapter 13

National Lampoon's CNY Vacation – Cambodia

"At this point I must have been averaging one 'bad decision I didn't have to face the consequences of' per day."

Growing up in America gives you a narrow perspective on freedom. Freedom to you means voting and saying [insert political party or irrelevant bureaucrat here] is stupid on Facebook. That a cop dressed in combat gear like he's marching on Fallujah will arrest an 18-year-old for drinking a beer in his parent's backyard, or that you can get a ticket for jaywalking across an empty street doesn't make you reconsider the idea of freedom. Living in China, your concept of freedom changes. I may not be able to call the government stupid on the internet, but when was that ever useful anyway? And here no one cares if 17-year-old me walks across three lanes of active traffic with a fifth of vodka and a pack of cigarettes. It's a difference of at what level society wants to be strict on enforcement.

America is puritan micro-management, extremely strict on matters of day-to-day life. But you get big, idealistic freedoms. Speech, worship, guns, the like.

Chinese freedom is the opposite. Day-to-day life is more or less unregulated; there aren't a million little rules to follow to ensure you're compliant with the latest complicated regulation designed solely to extract money from you. The Western image of daily life in China for the average Chinese — bleak and repressive, timid before the awesome might of the central government, who stands ready to pounce if you so much as think the wrong thought — is absurd and wrong. The average person walking down the street in Beijing feels bowed to no one. The Chinese are a belligerent people, and I mean that as a sincere compliment.

In this sense, I think American and Chinese freedom can both rightfully be called freedom, or degrees of freedom, but they are polar opposites of each other. Russia is probably like China. Europe is somewhere in between the two.

But then you go to a place like Cambodia and you realize there's a third kind of freedom. Pure freedom. What "freedom" most likely meant to people before the 20th century. Where day-to-day life is unregulated, business regulations are basic and straightforward, and while grand ideals like freedom of speech may not be formally guaranteed, they're functional realities since government enforcement is haphazard at any level. On the off-chance a traffic cop cares enough to get off his ass, $50 directly to his pocket makes him look the other way on any violation. They have no Second Amendment, yet as I walk through the red-light district, there's a random man napping on the side of the road in a folding chair with an AK-47 strewn across his lap.

    The law is whatever is enforced. America enforces the little things, ensnares you in the minutiae. China enforces the big things. Some places enforce nothing, be it for lack of organization or lack of f*cks to give. Cambodia enforces nothing, and that's where I found myself over Chinese New Year 2018, scouting new opportunities for Michael.

    After my friend Matt came out to Shanghai in the beginning of February, I wanted to find a way to get him involved in the project and secure himself a position like I had the year before. Chinese New Year was coming up, which meant that Shanghai would become a ghost town for about two weeks while everyone went home for the holiday. I wanted to go somewhere warm and have a good time instead of being bored in Shanghai. When I was in Fuzhou the previous month, one of our billionaire friends kept going on about how much opportunity there was in Cambodia. He had all sorts of projects going there, from casinos to factories to infrastructure. I'd been to Thailand before and liked it. Figured I'd probably like Cambodia too.

    Cambodia's not Thailand, though. Its recent history is dark. It's much poorer and less developed than Thailand. I couldn't get an accurate read on what to expect. The internet alternated between people saying it was very dangerous and people saying it was similar to Thailand. I was bored with familiar, nice places like Taipei and Tokyo, so the aspect of having a bit of an adventure definitely made it more interesting. James told me he read you can shoot a cow with a rocket launcher. I booked my tickets.

    Matt and I flew down to Phnom Penh, the capital of Cambodia, a day or two into CNY. Got in late. Had an Airbnb booked in an apartment complex that didn't have an exact address. We told the cab driver the street at the airport. He took us to a different street. Found a tuk tuk driver who knew the street we meant, but he wanted three dollar. No, one dollar. Ok ok one dollar. Took us to the correct street. Eventually found the apartment building and went to bed.

    The first day was uneventful but fun. Checking the place out, I rented a motor scooter and handed over my passport as collateral. Bad decision I didn't have to face the consequences of. We went down to the red-light district in the afternoon. Not interesting before nightfall. Just women getting their makeup on in the middle of the street while my guy with the AK naps nearby. The Western food in Cambodia is surprisingly good. There are tons of Europeans and Americans there, but they're mostly whackos — even a different breed from the ones you find in Thailand. Some backpackers too.

    We went back to the red-light district after dinner. One of the go-go bars has a second-floor deck that overlooks the entire street and all the other bars. We posted up there with our beers for some people watching, took over the stereo in the bar and blasted our own favorites throughout the place. Matt chatted up a Cambodian hooker and reenacted the scene from *The Big Short* where Steve Carrell asks a stripper about the housing market. She gave surprisingly good advice.

The next morning I woke up in one of those moods where you just want to shoot a cow with a rocket-propelled grenade. I asked the doorman of the apartment if that was a real thing. He said he wasn't so sure about the cow anymore, but he'd take us out to the base and see what we could do. We set out on a tuk tuk, Matt, the doorman, and me. Drove for about an hour. The doorman said we'd get to the military base soon, but they won't let us in without a small bribe. I was ready for him to say it'd be a few hundred dollars. A pack of cigarettes would suffice, apparently. I can afford that.

Sure enough, the sentries at the gate to the base were very pleased with their new cigarettes. They let us in. People helping people. We drove over to the base's shooting range and met an officer. I asked if we could shoot the RPG. He said yes but we have to drive to another range in the mountains, no shooting the RPG at this base. One shot of the RPG would cost $400, and I have to pick other things to shoot too, otherwise he doesn't feel it's worth his time. Fine. I picked three other guns: a belt-fed machine gun, an AK, and a Vietnam-era M16. I asked about the cow. No more cow. He asked if I wanted to throw a hand-grenade for $100. I declined. In addition to the cost of the weapons, he wanted $30 for gas to drive us round-trip to the mountain range. I agreed.

We got in his truck and drove nearly two hours out into the Cambodian countryside. On the way we drove by a lot of factories. The system was explained to me: Despite its prevalence, prostitution is technically illegal, and on occasion they round up a group of hookers and arrest them. That's the trap of "the law is what's enforced" — when something is illegal but not enforced, until all of a sudden it is, and then you're screwed. Anyway, it was common practice to staff factories in Cambodia by arresting hookers and giving them a choice: work in the factories indefinitely, for 12 to 15 hours a day and $30 a month, or go to prison. This is how your clothes are made.

    The countryside was actually very beautiful compared to the dirty inner city. It was surreal, sitting in the back of a Cambodian officer's truck, driving through the countryside listening to Cambodian pop music over the radio, watching the scenery. We eventually got to the shooting range, which was just the side of a mountain with the brush cleared out. Unpacked the guns. First up, the RPG.

    If an RPG is not properly maintained, it can blow up when you try to fire it, making your head disappear. I did not trust the Cambodians to properly maintain their weapons. It was slightly nerve-racking. I figured there was a chance I'd be dead in a second, but I wasn't going to not fire it — I'd come all this way. I fired it at the mountain, watched the explosion, and all the Cambodian officers (there were a few more at the range) sarcastically cheered. The other guns weren't so interesting. The belt-fed jammed every other shot and had to be manually charged like it was a bolt-action. Waste of $100. The M16 worked fine but isn't special. The AK was surprising. It did what I was afraid the RPG would do. I stepped up, took my first shot, and it exploded. The upper receiver flew straight into my forehead right above my eye. Probably should've been wearing eye protection. At this point I must have been averaging at least one serious "bad decision I didn't have to face the consequences of" per day.

All in all, the shooting took less than ten minutes and cost almost $1,000. I told the officer we were ready to leave and he pulled a live grenade out of his pocket. I guess he put it there when we were at the first base. I told him I didn't want to throw the grenade. He started yelling at me, saying he already took it from the base so I had to pay for it. Now I got angry. *I already spent a ton of money and told you at the base I didn't want it. I'm not using it or paying for it.* He backed down, said fine, and put the grenade back in his pocket. He demanded another $50 to drive back. I started arguing again, which he didn't like. The local doorman from our apartment, who was still accompanying us, looked at me like I was crazy. I took that as a sign I should just pay the $50.

Another two hours back through the Cambodian countryside and we arrived at the officer's house, where our tuk tuk was waiting to take us back into town. We got back to the apartment in the evening. I cleaned the oil and gunpower from my face. Apparently having a gun explode in your face gets it a bit dirty. I was both very pleased and annoyed that I had spent a bit over $1,000 to shoot an RPG at a mountain and almost lose an eye to fire 100 shots out of guns I've shot before. I settled on being content with the experience and planned to go to the casino and try to win the money back.

Matt and I went to the casino to play poker. We'd both been decent at poker playing with friends in high school. Actually, he was very good, I was just decent. We both bought into a game of Texas Hold 'Em for probably $100 each. Six other players of various nationalities were at the table. Next to us was an older Australian expat. Across the table was a guy from Macau who didn't speak English. I bankrupted him 20 minutes into the game. Matt went bankrupt a bit after that, not by my hand. I didn't make back all the money, but I did win $200 and took Matt out to the club to celebrate.

The next day we went to look at some condos for sale. I had a friend in Thailand who'd made some money with that kind of investment and it was popular on the internet, so I thought we should check it out. There may have been some good deals out there, but what we saw looked like a bad deal to me. Studio apartments in sunny Phnom Penh, Cambodia, for $70,000-$100,000. A lot of unfinished projects trying to get you in super early, even before they'd broken ground. I think there was definitely potential in these trades, but we were being shown the wrong projects; on a tour for people with a superficial understanding of the market, who'd read it was a "good trade" online. Which was me. I tried to see if I could get a look at some of the other ventures that I knew existed in Cambodia, but I didn't have good enough contacts and it just didn't pan out.

After a week and a half we returned to Shanghai empty handed. No projects to recommend to Michael. Didn't really learn any lessons from it either. Don't go to a new place in search of projects without proper contacts set up beforehand, maybe? Don't go out into the boonies with Cambodian army officers if you're going to get heated over a $50 dispute? It was a lot of fun, but I don't feel a strong urge to go back.

Chapter 14

Stress Dreams

I had the dream again. Third time this month. Typical to have it every week or two. Everyone has stress dreams, I'm no different. I perform extremely well under pressure in the waking world, but I still feel stress, sometimes copious amounts of it, and some experiences have left an impression on me that I can't shake. So I've had the same recurring stress dream, almost once a week, for the last three years.

There are some pretty universal stress dreams. It's the middle of the night and someone breaks into your house. They're going to kill you. You take aim with your gun and all of a sudden there's a thousand-pound trigger pull. Finally squeeze a shot off. Nothing happens. Maybe the gun melts in your hands. I've had this one. Freaky tooth problems are another common stress dream. I've had those too.

Lots of people say they get recurring stress dreams about school. My parents told me I'd get them. It's the morning before a test and you forgot to study. Show up to school

Stress Dreams

unprepared. You're naked. That kind of thing. They were right that I'd get school stress dreams. But mine are a bit different. I can't have stress dreams about a test because I've never felt stress over taking a test — or just about any school assignment, for that matter. So my stress dreams aren't about tests.

Every week or so, right on schedule, someone tells me. *Bill, the state just passed a new law — you have to go back for one more year of high school.* How can that be? I've been out of school for years. I'm an adult. They can't make me go back. Oh yes they can. I'm back in the classroom. All my former classmates are there. I'm the only one outraged for some reason. *Just cheer up man, it's gonna be fun.* Are you kidding?

Now I'm really back. Back in an environment of ritual embarrassment for young men. Twenty-one-year-old me, being browbeaten by a 25-year-old woman because I refuse to sit in a circle and tell the class what animal I'd be if I could pick any animal (no, I'm not exaggerating, this did really happen both in high school *and college orientation*). The same condescension, the same arbitrary punishment, the same monotony, the same losers, the same teachers staring at 14-year-old-girl-in-yoga-pants ass. I'm going to go insane.

I try to find a place to hide. How can I be living like this after how I lived the last few years in Asia? I can't hide. I'm scolded for going somewhere without permission. Every dream ends the same way. Approximately the same way I actually ended high school. A crescendo of white rage building inside, f*ck you I won't do what you tell me repeated over and over in my head, starting at a whisper and ending in me actually screaming it out loud, like *Rage Against the Machine*. A teacher asks why I didn't do the homework. I snap. Dream fades out as I cuss out the given teacher of the week and either storm off or get dragged off by the police for being an unruly student. I wake up. It's ok, Bill, you graduated high school years ago.

Chapter 15

Oligarchs, Diamonds, and Bankers – Mauritius

"Apparently Vietnam was becoming a new investment favorite for global oligarchs. Too bad I wasted my time in Cambodia on the advice of mere billionaires."

Even as the stamped pages in my passport were ballooning in lockstep with the crypto market, I hadn't originally considered Africa part of the play. We had planned to go to Mauritius, an African island country, in January but cancelled last minute due to hurricanes. There was also an epidemic of the plague in nearby Madagascar, which slightly dampened my enthusiasm, but Michael had been out there with Mary the previous year, and they'd made some solid contacts on the island. There were a lot of potential projects to be done, both crypto and otherwise.

Our main contact on the island was a man named Hudson. Hudson used to help run the African arm of a large multinational banking group out of South Africa and was now living in Mauritius running his own firm. I'd originally started working with him the previous November, when Michael began sending everyone who wanted their own coin my way. He had a friend who wanted a coin for his contract-for-difference "CFD" trading platform — similar to binary options in that they are basically gamified derivatives, the line between gambling product and financial product extremely blurry. The deal was simple: we help them get a CFD coin, they would help Michael set up a prawn farm in Mauritius, an idea he was obsessed with at the time.

Hudson was one of the first people Michael ever sent my way, so I leveled with him that this "new coin" business was being done on the fly. He didn't care at all. He was getting tons of interest from his network in doing all sorts of different coins and thought there was huge potential in us building out the business out together. I'd handle coin production and he'd handle the business side, garnering clients from his network across Africa and Europe. Sounded like a great plan to me, and over the course of the next few months we communicated constantly and worked to build out various projects for his network.

Within a week of getting back from Cambodia, at the end of Chinese New Year, Michael let me know the Mauritius trip was on again. Not only were he and I going to meet with Hudson and all of our recently acquired clients for the new coin business, but much of the team from both Europe and Shanghai was invited to come hold meetings for two weeks. It was not the most logical destination to fly that many people out for meetings, but nobody was complaining about having a warm place to go in February.

    I started planning how I'd get there. Michael was already in Mauritius when he told me to come. It's a 10-hour direct flight from Shanghai, and I knew Michael wouldn't cover first class airfare at the time. That didn't work for me. So I flew to Singapore first, which is only a five-hour flight. Coach on Singapore Airlines is nicer than first class on United in America, so it was fine. I spent one day and night in Singapore. Stayed at the Westin, which happened to be a brand-new property with big rooms. Nice for a night. The nonstop travel, Cambodia to Singapore to Mauritius in just a few weeks, in peak crypto bubble where our project's coin had gone from $3 to $50 in a month, had me spending quite freely. During my 20 hours in Singapore, I went to very nice restaurants, bought some jewelry, and went out drinking by myself, which I don't even enjoy that much.

    The next day I boarded what I thought was my Singapore Airlines flight to Mauritius. I found out it was actually operated by Air Mauritius. The plane was much older than the Singapore Airlines fleet and being in that coach for seven hours was a pain. I'm a brat, though.

    I landed in Mauritius at night. A customs officer grabbed my luggage for me off the baggage claim and started asking me why I was there. Great, not 10 minutes into entering

Africa and I'm getting shaken down. My experience with the Cambodian officers had taught me that trying to stand your ground in a foreign country doesn't always pan out. In these situations, you have to make a quick assessment of what you really have control over, and more importantly what they control, and play your hand accordingly. So I shrugged, said I was a student, and he let me go.

My cab from the airport to the hotel took another two hours and cost $150. Along the way I found out that people in Mauritius like to drive straight down the middle of their winding, two-way, jungle/mountain roads. I checked into the resort where our project's team was staying, then went to find Michael. He and his wife were eating dinner. Joined them for a drink and went to bed.

In the morning I finally met Hudson in person. He let me in on the plan for my time in Mauritius. First, we'd meet his friend, an Italian, who was allegedly one of the biggest diamond traders in Africa. He was considering a 'Diamond Coin' and wanted our consultation. Then we'd meet Mauritius' very own oligarchs, the main powerful family of the island, who were one of his clients. They didn't want a coin; Hudson just wanted to connect us with them in case we ended up going through with the prawn farm. At some point, we'd have a call with the "Yacht Coin" people, a group of bankers who owned a fleet of yachts and were hoping to expand their fleet by raising money via an ICO. Of course, there were also a lot of new team members here from Europe that I was to meet with on matters directly related to our own project.

Oligarchs, Diamonds, and Bankers – Mauritius

I spent the first few days lounging at the resort with Michael while the rest of the team trickled in from Shanghai, London, and a few other places in Europe. The Thomas situation with the hit piece climaxed at this time, and Michael was mostly complaining about that to me. Otherwise he was explaining the operational details of a prawn farm or talking about Kitty Cash. The lead developer for Kitty Cash was flying in from Germany and brought us Kitty Cash merch, shirts, stickers, whatnot. We opened bidding for Kitty Cash cats via our online communities. People who'd bought into the original Crypto Kitties cats on Ethereum had made tens of thousands of dollars flipping them. I guess some people thought they'd do the same with the Kitty Cash cats. The first cat auctioned stalled at a half Bitcoin bid with two minutes left. Michael told me to throw out a .75 Bitcoin bid and see if I could send it into a last-minute frenzy. I did, and everyone went nuts, bidding over each other through the final 90 seconds. Someone ultimately paid just over a Bitcoin (around $10,000) as the winning bid for their cat concept.

Once the rest of the team arrived, we began meetings. The goal was to define a formal organizational structure, which we lacked, and develop a new Western marketing plan now that it was clear Thomas and his people were headed out.

Michael flew out a new guy from the States to join the marketing team. He'd originally just been a very active community member in the chatrooms, but he convinced Michael to fly him out and put him to work. A male model. We'll call him *Zoolander*. Zoolander only spent a day trying to get a feel for the team structure before asserting himself at the top of it. It was a light-speed version of the already quick title changing that Thomas had maneuvered. New guy to marketing director to CMO within one meeting. Michael didn't allow it. That slowed him down temporarily.

    One of our programmers got sick within a day of being there. No problem, just a typical cold. Then he started having seizures and was unconscious. Then everyone else felt like they had a cold. I was resigned to the fact that I now had the plague in Africa. Why did I come here? But it turned out that we really did just have colds and the programmer had some weird other thing (not the plague) that resolved itself after a few days. Lucky.

    The team meetings were a drag and didn't really require my presence. As the other team members were very happy to present, I didn't have a clear place in the new organizational chart they made. I didn't belong to marketing, or development, or whatever. I just belonged to Michael. I was his right-hand man, which doesn't really work on an organizational chart. Zoolander seemed especially giddy to present that fact, and that he was now was higher up as the "Marketing Director". I stopped going to the meetings. It was either status-based infighting or designing the new website, and I wanted no part in either. Organizational charts meant nothing to me since I knew they meant nothing to Michael. Formal structures aside, he clearly still decided his underlings' authority and compensation based on his personal relationship with them, and other than James, no one was closer to him than me.

Oligarchs, Diamonds, and Bankers – Mauritius

Finally, Hudson gave us the green light for the meetings. One morning while the rest of the team argued over each other's titles, Hudson drove Michael and me over to a bay on the western coast of the island to meet the oligarchs in their villa. Biggest meeting I'd had to date, and I felt like I had the flu. Had to push through it. I was on top of my game, feeling like death aside.

Their villa was beautiful, right on the water. We were invited to sit in their living room. The three of us sat there and talked for an hour or so with two generations of Mauritian power — the elderly head of family and his two sons, as well as their banker, who I think was Hudson's original connection to them. They told good stories. Originally they had power in both Mauritius and Seychelles, until they ended up on the wrong side of a coup in Seychelles and left to consolidate in Mauritius. The family who owned Madagascar, friends of theirs, moved to Mauritius because they kept getting kidnapped in Madagascar. Even after being kidnapped multiple times and moving, they recently had a shipment get held up in Madagascar, went back to handle it, and, sure enough, got kidnapped (they could barely get this story out; they were laughing so hard, they cried). They were generally pleased with the current president of Mauritius but were considering swapping him for another guy just to spice things up. Didn't matter, they owned both of them anyway.

They explained the politics and structure of Mauritius, how to do business here, how to do business in various countries of the African mainland, and reiterated that we should absolutely not go to Madagascar. There will be no talking animals, just kidnappers.

They also talked to us about some of the projects they had outside of Africa. Apparently Vietnam was becoming a new investment favorite for global oligarchs. Too bad I wasted my time in Cambodia on the advice of mere billionaires.

We left the villa happy with the meeting but without any concrete plan to do anything with these people. They'd offered assistance with the prawn farm and in developing government contacts, but Michael wasn't totally committed to the idea yet despite his constant raving about it. Both of us were mainly just fascinated by the stories they told.

Next we drove back up the island to meet with the diamond trader. Our meeting with him was less stories and more business. We got there around noon. His wife had made lunch, and we all talked over pasta and wine. He wasn't exactly sure how his trade could have anything to do with a theoretical coin, why he'd need it, or why he should pay for our services in making it, but he knew that people were raising a hundred million dollars for nothing, so he may as well learn about it.

I wasn't exactly sure how to fit a coin to his business, either. I tried to be creative. I've seen people with a lot less of a business than this guy force a coin into the world. But this seemed to need real forcing. I presented him with some ideas on the fly. Michael wasn't involved in the talk — the spotlight was on Hudson and me — so he moved to the couch and was reading something on his phone that was apparently hilarious, since he kept giggling.

Oligarchs, Diamonds, and Bankers – Mauritius

We came up with some decent ideas of how to work a coin into the trader's business, but he clearly sensed it was a bit of a stretch. He wasn't wrong. He told us if we could show him sufficient interest in one of our concepts from the market, he'd do a deal with us. Sounded fair. We left it at that.

We met back up with the rest of the team at the resort. Hudson let everyone know that he'd scheduled an outing for us that afternoon. He'd hired a boat from the harbor to sail us out into the ocean for a couple hours. The boat was stocked with beer, liquor, and snacks. I was still feeling sick, but it was a beautiful day and everyone else was going, so I went as well. We got on the boat and sailed out into the Indian Ocean, in a straight line, for a few hours, then sailed straight back. The scenery was incredible. I knew if I drank it'd make me sick for another two or three days at least, but I also knew I'd never be on a party boat headed straight into the Indian Ocean with my friends in Africa ever again, so I went ahead and got blasted, sat on the bow, and talked shit with everyone.

On the way back a few of us decided, in our drunken state, that we should totally go to the casino. But we had to go back to the hotel and get dressed up first, for some reason. Of course, when we got back to the hotel it was nighttime and no one wanted to move again. Coincidentally, the hotel set up a poker game next to the bar. So Zoolander, a couple programmers from London and I joined the game. A few German guys also sat down to play. We ordered more drinks and got into it. The hotel didn't allow real money gambling, so it was just for fun, but we took it seriously. I was getting absolutely crushed, but when the dealer called last hand, he said whoever wins this hand wins the game. Everyone went all-in before the deal. I was dealt AK suited, won the hand and thus the game. Woohoo. I knew I was good at poker.

    I asked what I won and the dealer/hotel bartender said nothing, it's just for fun. Bullshit. I started breaking his balls. He said he'd see what he could do. Came back with a bottle of champagne. Drank with everyone who'd played. Fun day. The last one that I'd have in Mauritius.

    Nothing bad happened after that, just nothing of note happened either. I've never been big on beachside resorts, so the novelty of that was lost on me after the first day there. There are no towns within walking distance, so to go into the city you'd have to pay $100-plus for a cab and risk your life on the Mauritian roads. Instead, you eat in the hotel. Resort food, minimum $40 per meal. Extremely mediocre. Add on the fact that you're not in Asia receiving the best service on the planet, you're in Africa — ethnically French/Indian Africa, at that — receiving what must be the worst service on the planet. And I'm still sick, and still bored, and the meetings I needed to attend are done.

    After being there for two weeks, I finally flew back to Shanghai in the first week of March. Misread my departure time and got to the Mauritian airport five hours before my flight. Mauritian service quality at least kept me busy with check in and security at an empty airport for the first hour, but still I sat there for hours before finally boarding my 10-hour Air Mauritius flight. Luckily I had convinced Michael to pony up for first-class airfare this time.

In the days before leaving, I talked at length with Hudson. We would keep in constant contact after I was back in China. I drafted a pricing plan for him that put our coin production services around $50,000 a pop. Our costs would be around $10,000. He laughed and said we could easily charge over $200,000. Great. He said he'd stay on top of the potential clients on his end, I just needed to stay ready to produce.

Chapter 16

Interim – March in Shanghai

"It was the first move I'd made that turned out badly ... they didn't give me as much free reign again."

Except for the few days between my Cambodia and Mauritius trips, I'd been out of China for more or less a month straight. Michael stayed in Mauritius and went on to conferences in Malta, Germany, and Puerto Rico before returning to China at the end of the month. I didn't want to tag along since the travel would be a massive pain. Big mistake.

    At the Malta conference, Michael sat on a panel with John McAfee, creator of the famous antivirus software and notorious fugitive. The panel was hyped as the conference's most exciting event — the two of them would face off and see who had the most outrageous stories. The conversation ended up being pretty tame. But McAfee and Michael talked afterwards and hit it off. He loved our project. Even got a tattoo of our logo on his spine. He invited Michael to stay at his

Interim – March in Shanghai

estate, and when he went a few months later, they shot at fish with machine guns off the side of McAfee's speedboat. Apparently McAfee walks around his own house with two guns, a pistol and an assault rifle, on him at all times. Doesn't stop smoking or drinking — ever. Undisputed, undefeated, worldwide party king. Wish I'd met him.

Back in Shanghai without Michael around, I didn't have much in the way of new tasks on a daily or even weekly basis. I hoped to take the opportunity to relax for the entire month, not traveling anywhere. That plan lasted a week and a half.

I was genuinely glad to be back in Shanghai. In my familiar apartment instead of a hotel, with my girlfriend, going to my usual coffee shops, having some semblance of a routine. But ten days in one city felt endless. I was itching to be back on the road where I was (and still am) most at home.

Before heading back out, I checked in with Matt. He hadn't gone to Mauritius with me. Even though I was bringing him in to the new coin business, I felt I couldn't justify asking Michael to spend ten grand for Matt to be there when they'd only met once or twice. I think I was the only person on the planet being careful with Michael's money, including himself.

I thought Matt would be kept busy in my absence. He'd come up with the idea to make a crypto casino based on our project's coin and got approval from Michael. In the two weeks I was gone he did work on it, but somehow his schedule had shifted from a normal wake up in the morning, go to sleep at night, to wake up at 8 p.m., sleep at 1 p.m. He was a bit of a wreck. This lifestyle can do that to you. Probably should have brought him to Mauritius, if for no other reason than to keep him from falling off track.

My family let me know they'd be coming to China in a week for my sister's spring break. I immediately took the opportunity to get back on the road. I mean, seriously, I hadn't been in an airport for almost two weeks. Insanity. I told my mom to fly out before the rest of the family and meet me in Taipei. Didn't do any business that time. No sweet crypto parties. Just coffee and food, walking around with my mom. It was very nice. I went back to Shanghai after a couple days while she stayed to wait for the rest of the family. They'd all meet me in Hangzhou a few days later. I realized there was a crypto conference being held in Hangzhou, and our project's local marketing team was already there. I took the next train down. So much for a month straight in Shanghai. The conference was held in the building they use for the G20 summit. I manned a booth to advertise our project. Local attendees thought they just hired me to stand there and be a white face since I couldn't yet speak good enough Chinese yet to talk about the project. It was a boring conference.

Spent a few days in Hangzhou with my family, then we went to Xiamen, China's Miami, for another few days then back to Shanghai. They went back to America.

Matt went back to America, too, so he could see his family. I heard no updates about the casino project for a while, and then the people he'd hired started bugging me about payment. Apparently, he wasn't communicating with them either. Matt eventually reached out to me and let me know he'd decided the project wasn't viable, and he'd pay the programmers from his own salary. He didn't end up coming back to Shanghai. For some reason, the programmers then went to James and explained how upset they were over the whole thing. It really wasn't a big deal, but since I brought Matt in and vouched for him, I was ultimately responsible. It was the first move I'd made that turned out badly, and I lost some credibility with James and Michael. It wasn't personal, but they didn't give me as much free reign again.

It didn't help that the crypto bubble was winding down, either. The air was being let out of the whole thing. Prices hadn't cratered yet, but their movement had ground to a halt. No more infinite gains. It wasn't clear whether this was a temporary break in the party or if the party was about to be over for good. I didn't know that in just over a week's time, the closing bell would ring.

Chapter 17

Closing Bell – Back in Tokyo

"… we'd also hired a Japanese crypto girl who, for a small sum, covered her entire body in our project's logo using custom temporary tattoos. She was our Japanese 'brand ambassador'."

There was a massive crypto conference in Tokyo set for the first week of April. The kind where the tickets cost thousands of dollars, there are thousands of people in attendance, and organizers plan all sorts of after-parties and 'VIP' dinners. Michael was friends with the guy who put the whole thing together, so our project would be involved with all of it at a heavy discount.

  Michael came back to Shanghai at the end of March and put me in charge of organizing how we'd handle the Tokyo conference. We had a Europe and North America team for Western conferences, and our other activities were focused in China with the Chinese team. We had no Japanese team, and it didn't make sense to fly people out from Europe or the US for a Japanese conference when we were right here in Shanghai. Michael had also been invited to be a main speaker at the event. We decided that Michael, James, and I would handle it ourselves. There were also a few expats in Tokyo who were in our community, and they volunteered to help man the booth.

I booked all of our flights and our hotel. The conference was held at the Westin, so I booked us there using my SPG rewards account that I'd been building up through all my recent travel. I would earn a ton of points on the trip and was excited. Scoring airline and hotel status had become an infatuation for me, and I hadn't been to Tokyo since my first business trip at the very beginning of the bubble. How many 18-year-old SPG platinum's can there be?

Through our volunteers, we organized a small meetup the night before the conference. We got to Tokyo in the afternoon, checked into the hotel, then headed back out to run the meetup. It was in a small office building near Shibuya, the famous shopping district and home to the world's busiest intersection. The meetup drew a crowd of around 30, all Japanese. We had a live translator, who politely requested Michael pause after every sentence or two to let him translate. That didn't work. It was a hard job.

I found out we'd also hired a Japanese crypto girl who, for a small sum, covered her entire body in our project's logo using custom temporary tattoos. She was our Japanese "brand ambassador", as they say, and even wore branded clothing. She stood at our booth every day at the conference to draw attention our way. After the meetup she took us out for sushi.

The conference the next day was boring, just like every other conference. We stood at the booth for hours, handing out t-shirts and explaining our project to people who politely pretended to listen while waiting for their turn to shill their own garbage. Collected business cards. Eventually it was time for Michael to give his speech. It was the biggest crowd he'd ever addressed. I expected him to give the same speech he'd given at every other conference, a dry but informative overview of our project's history, technology, and goals. Instead he got up and dove into an only slightly on-topic rant about how most everyone in the room was a scammer, how he was given thousands of Bitcoins just for being in the early chatrooms, and that he was working on fixing the problems of Bitcoin — which he described in detail, but failed to describe his proposed solutions. He also failed to discuss his own project. He mentioned the name of our project once, in a passive way, as if he was just vaguely familiar with it and not its creator. James and I stood in the back of the room laughing. Those standing near us were just confused.

While the conference was a bore, the after-parties were great, even better than what the guys in Taipei hosted. I mean, the go-to move was still just to rent out a bar, but these bars were nicer than the Taipei ones. Picture a rooftop bar overlooking Tokyo. Michael and I drank with the president of the North American Farmers association. He wanted to do a coin with us. Michael pitched him on some drone projects he'd been working on. It was less impressive to me when I realized that "North American" implied "not the USA." Why was he in

Tokyo, anyway? What's the connection between Japanese financial technology and Canadian farmers?

After the rooftop bar, we went downstairs and met with the conference organizer. He took us to another bar. Had some people he wanted us to meet. Another "market maker". We were told he used to be a big trader on Wall Street, but if you were actually a big trader on Wall Street, you'd have never left to be involved in crypto to begin with. When people said they were traders, they want you to think of Wall Street, but really they just mean they day traded from their home office. I asked this guy what he traded before getting into crypto. He named five different products, including binary options. Yep, a scammer. I let Michael know after we left. Didn't do business with him.

Next day, the conference was boring as expected. There was another after-party that night, different bar. Michael and James had been invited by the conference organizer to a VIP dinner with local exchanges. We still hadn't managed to get on any major exchanges, so this was an important dinner for them. They told me to go to the normal after-party and continue networking there. No problem.

I took the two volunteers from the booth to the after-party with me. It took me a while to get into social butterfly mode. The free-flowing drinks helped. I tried talking to a group of people, but a few of them were from a certain company (we'll call them "Company X"), flown out from New York (Brooklyn). Insufferable. They didn't like me either, since I wasn't part of their crowd, which was still seen as cool at the time. A year later people would tell you to f*ck off if they found out you were Company X. Most useless people around. The previous spring, when I was still in high school working on my own project, a family friend, former department head at the United Nations, reached out and expressed interest in incorporating Ethereum/blockchain into a project he was working on with some peers. Former UN people. They wanted to use blockchain to empower an open-source market for funding violence-prevention projects in the developing world. A too-good-to-be-true dream for anyone looking to make a PR buzz in the industry and I handed it to Company X on a platter. My friend had already designed the concept but needed technical info to present to his peers at the end of the month. I put him in touch with my contact at Company X, who said not to worry, he'd get my friend everything he needed very soon. Kept stalling and stalling and eventually disappeared. My friend's blockchain concept fell through as a result. I'd fallen for the marketing that they were the *serious* guys really *getting things done* in the space. I thought I was just unlucky, but over time I heard nothing but the same kind of story from an ever-increasing amount of people. Eventually anyone who actually wanted to get work done avoided them.

  Even though it was still early I was already pretty drunk, and ended up in a haze where I met around 10 people in two minutes. Open one person, he introduces me to his friend who says *oh you know who you just have to meet* and introductions and introductions and introductions. You can't forget someone's name if you didn't listen to what it was in the first place. Luckily for me the last person I was introduced to was worthwhile. She was a PR girl, ran her own firm. Not sure if she actually had business going or not. We hit it off, probably because she was interested in getting me as a client. I talked with her and the guy she was originally talking with, a forty-something Swiss-French guy whose involvement in crypto was unclear. Oh, he's an investor. Whatever that means.

We all had a good time talking and drinking. She offered to take the two of us out for a night on the town. She said she was Queen of Roppongi, Tokyo's seedy party district, and could show us the best Tokyo had to offer. Eighteen-year-old me and the Swiss-French investor, a walking stereotype of the middle-aged European playboy, took her up on it. I was still underage, drinking age in Tokyo being 20, but if I was really with the *Queen* of Roppongi I figured she could manage a way around it.

We went out to eat. Izakaya. Endless skewers of various meats and seafood. Beer and music. Swiss guy getting handsy. Absolutely stuffed. We walk outside and down the street, her friend owns a small karaoke bar nearby. Right outside the bar I run into the woman who bought me a non-alcoholic beer on my first business trip. What are the odds? She'd just gotten back to Tokyo that day. She was with her boyfriend. I invited them to drink with us. Real alcohol this time. We sat in the karaoke bar knocking back cocktails and talking while the Queen of Roppongi sang her heart out. Her friends came. Three guys. Twenty-year-old Japanese college dropouts turned businessmen, wearing fine Japanese suits and diamond jewelry. My people.

Their English was just good enough to let me know how much they love Eminem. Really my people.

The Queen eventually let us know it was time to go to her dominion — Roppongi. I was slightly anxious since I was likely to be shut out of the clubs, but I rolled with it for the time being. We left the bar and found a stretch limo waiting for us. No idea when she called for it. Nice surprise. Got in the limo and drank champagne as we rolled towards Roppongi. I now decided to tell the Queen, not that I was underage, but that I wasn't carrying I.D. She reminded me that she was, in fact, the Queen of Roppongi and would not be fazed by such a small problem. I was not to worry. But the first club we went to refused to let me in. Everyone seemed a bit annoyed with me. No problem, said the Queen, and we got back in the limo and were taken to another club. They didn't card, and had a booth waiting for us. More champagne. I was regressing. Non-verbal. Eventually ended up back in the hotel room. In between is hazy. Never saw any of them again.

I slept through the third day. Not sure why we didn't leave that day, nothing more to accomplish in Tokyo, but a lot to do in Shanghai — we were organizing our own conference there just a couple days later. We had a final sushi meal then left the next morning.

I didn't know it yet, but the bubble had just burst. Tokyo was the closing bell. It ended climactically and poetically — the perfect business trip, masterfully combining work and play, in absolutely over-the-top fashion, in the very place I had

Closing Bell – Back in Tokyo

my first-ever business trip. Stuck the landing. I'm an artist. But everything would go quickly downhill from here.

Chapter 18

Cracks Begin to Show

"It didn't pan out. Nothing panned out."

What made crypto work was that despite the prevalence of scammers, there was always a core base of hyper-dedicated hobbyists. Calling them hobbyists doesn't quite do them justice. Cryptocurrency was more than a hobby to them, it was an ideology, the natural conclusion of internet libertarianism for the technologically inclined. Some of the best programmers and technical minds in the world made up their ranks. Before the bubble, almost all of the people involved in crypto were like this. Almost no marketing/PR types. By the time we had our Shanghai conference the second week of April, the dedicated core was outnumbered by scammers and marketers 10,000 to 1.

Other than Michael and James, there wasn't a single serious programmer at our conference in Shanghai. They were all marketers, media people, journalists. "Influencers" from the US and China, who wanted to be paid to make the occasional

Cracks Begin to Show

video or Facebook post about your project for their (mostly fake) audience of subscribers. Still more people with the same scam "market making" proposal. Michael doing deals with these people and selling them a million in coin at half the market, then turning around and complaining to James and me that the exchange price is trending down.

  We finally got on an exchange. The biggest one. One of the Chinese marketing team members went to college with one of their higher-ups. That connection gave us the privilege of being permitted to pay two million dollars in Bitcoin plus some obscene amount of our own coin to be listed. Not to be listed immediately, or promoted whatsoever, but to be dicked around for a couple months while the launch date was postponed repeatedly for unspecified reasons. When we finally did get listed there was a big rally and I made $75,000 in the first ten minutes of trading. I forgave their belligerence.

  Team morale was poor. The programmers were having difficulty getting clear instructions from Michael. He'd give them vague, big-picture plans, but no detail how to build properly. His focus was being pulled in a million different directions. He really didn't have the time to sit down and make clear plans for everyone. The Chinese marketing team was getting tired of seeing him blow infinite amounts of money in scams and seemingly unnecessary side projects while not getting particularly big salaries themselves. Only the Western marketing team was happy, because they were brand new. Zoolander was fired by James not long after Mauritius because he didn't bother to mask the fact he was only concerned with leveraging involvement in the project for his own personal gain. Once he'd gotten his face out there via an interview or two, he tried to promote himself not as our employee, but as an expert consultant that we'd been eager to contract. He was replaced with an external firm from the US. I met them for the first time at our Shanghai conference. Genuinely good guys. Michael complained they were expensive, but I never got into the details on it.

Michael opened a new "hardware office" in Shanghai to develop hardware related to the project, as well as for his own personal pet projects. Satellite discs, routers, personal computers, that sort of thing. He offered that I could manage the new office, then he flew out a different 18-year-old from Germany he found in our online chatroom to do it. My focus was becoming erratic, too. I was vexed. I wanted to run the hardware office. But wait, I don't know anything about electronics. How could I oversee the production of products I don't understand whatsoever? Let me on the marketing team. But the marketing team wants to force me to work out of their office, and it would separate me from directly reporting to Michael. My time as his right-hand-man was coming to an end.

What put the last nail in my coffin was failing to deliver on a new business line Michael and I had come up with on the flight to Fuzhou in January. Dirty electricity filters. Poor wiring in your house emits "dirty electricity", basically a type of radiation that has all sorts of adverse health effects. We made filters that you plug into the wall and it makes the problem go

Cracks Begin to Show

away. We had 100 prototypes made. They worked. He put me in charge of the business.

In early May I flew to Singapore and registered the company. Why did I need to open a company in Singapore? Not sure, I just read that's what smart people do. Spent a few thousand dollars to do that. On the way back from Singapore I stopped by Taipei and got my consultant friends to invite Charlie's company to speak about their products at a conference they were holding. I came back to Shanghai and wasn't sure how to manage making the filters, so I focused on the website. Hired some part-time guy to build it based on my basic designs. It didn't pan out. Nothing panned out. I wasn't on top of things anymore. The bubble had destroyed my work ethic. Working in the bubble was networking at after-parties, drunk off my ass. Working now was having the discipline to sit and focus, force an employee to finish the f*cking website already, and figure out how to mass produce filters. I didn't do any of that. I just stalled and stalled and eventually Michael called me out on it. Asked me straight up whether or not I felt I was fit to continue. I said I wasn't, I'd go join the marketing team instead. I don't remember exactly when that conversation happened, but it was the exact moment I lost my status as Michael's go-to guy. I think he was pretty disappointed, but other, more urgent matters came up and made him forget our issues in the short-term.

Michael had been very loose with accounting. If I or anyone else needed an expense covered, for a conference, a trip, a business dinner, whatever, we'd just send him a message with the amount, and he'd send us the money. He kept no records. He just didn't delete his messages. The messages were the accounts.

At some point he hired an actual accountant to go through his messages, and any formal accounts that other employees happened to keep, to try to make sense of them. She was good. Got a clear picture of the accounts together fairly quickly. It wasn't a pretty picture. The Chinese marketing team that was always envious of scammers making more money off Michael than they did while they working for him? They decided to become scammers themselves. Over the course of the previous six months they took advantage of his poor (non-existent) accounting practices and defrauded him of just over two million dollars. Compensation for trips that didn't happen. Coins for OTC deals that never went through. Salaries for fake team members. They'd been doing it for months and no one had noticed.

Since I was on the outs with Michael, I didn't know any of this was going on until James told me one night. I asked what they planned to do. They hadn't decided yet. They'd keep the team, four people in total, around for the time being and watch how they act. As far as the team was concerned, they were still safe and undetected in their scam. The next few weeks passed uneventfully — they kept working, Michael and James kept watching. I think they may have been tipped off to our suspicions as requests for approval for various new business trips were denied. One of them confronted Michael and demanded she be paid two million dollars' worth of our coin

Cracks Begin to Show

for her services rendered the last two years. She felt she'd brought more than enough value to the team to justify that.

James eventually decided he wanted to force a confrontation, but three out of four of the team were suddenly nowhere to be seen. Their leader was officially around but kept making excuses as to why he couldn't meet with James one-on-one. Bear in mind, James is a big guy who screams at people when angry, and everyone on this team was afraid of him. Even if they had no clue James suspected them, they'd be reluctant to meet if they detected any dissatisfaction on James's part.

As the team continued to duck James, I was more or less unemployed, attending occasional meetings just so I wasn't bored at home. In the first week of June, my dad came to visit.

Chapter 19

Lashing Out

"Get ready to go. Now."

My dad and I flew to Chongqing to eat spicy food, and I got intermittent updates on the situation in Shanghai from James. He still couldn't get any of the marketing team to meet in person. Meanwhile, the (new) marketing team under Michael's wife's direction let me know there was a big investor in Chongqing, and they'd appreciate if I would meet him for dinner and talk about the project. I added his WeChat. Local guy. He and his wife would take me out for hot pot. My Chinese was just good enough at this point that I felt comfortable being our project's spokesperson for the night. They picked me up and took me to the restaurant. As usual, it's China, so he ordered copious amounts of alcohol. We drank it all. Both hammered, we hadn't talked about the project for more than five minutes, instead talked about random stuff. I think he was just entertained to have a foreigner around. Asked

Lashing Out

if I liked Chinese girls. Sure, why not? He said next time I come let him know, he'll share his wife's friends with me. Told him I was amazed at the friendliness of the people in Chongqing.

We flew back to Shanghai. My dad planned to stay for another week or so before heading to the States. Maybe we'd travel to another nearby city, maybe stay in Shanghai. The night I got back, James told me they had identified and frozen all the accounts where the marketing team held stolen coins. Where they had money in exchange accounts, James contacted the exchanges and let them know it was stolen money. I asked if he'd heard from anyone on the team. Total radio silence on both sides.

I am paranoid by nature and tend to automatically imagine the worst possible outcome of any situation. Upon hearing they'd frozen all the stolen money, I asked James if he thought they might lash out violently. He didn't think it was a serious possibility. They've already committed a massive crime, why dig a deeper hole?

Michael and his wife came over to our apartment that night and stayed late to discuss the problems at hand. Went home after 1 a.m. I spent the next day hanging out with my dad and didn't think much about the situation. In the evening, he and I went to dinner. The whole time, walking to dinner, eating dinner, and after dinner, I felt incredibly uneasy. Like I was expecting to get sucker punched at any second, but it wasn't coming. I envisioned something going wrong with the marketing team situation, but what exactly could go wrong, I wasn't sure. I told my dad my concerns and he didn't think any escalation was likely.

After dinner I went back to my apartment where James and my girlfriend were waiting. I kept talking with James about the situation, how they wanted to handle it. Around 11:30, James noticed Michael's wife sent some of the evidence they'd been collecting in a group chat with the marketing team. James, confused and angry, *why would she send it to them?* He tried calling her, but she wouldn't answer. Neither of us thought much of it, just that she must have some poorly thought-out plan. We went to sleep.

I woke up at 7 a.m. and strolled out into the living room. James must have heard me come out and followed quickly behind with his phone in hand and an expression even more serious than usual. He was already speaking as he came through his bedroom door:

> *Pack a bag now, we have to leave immediately. They went to Michael's house last night, beat him and his wife, threatened to kill him, and somehow stole some Bitcoin. Said they're gonna come here next.*

I got a massive adrenaline rush, walked back into my room, and woke my girlfriend.

Get ready to go. Now.

Why?

Just do it.

Michael's apartment was maybe 30 minutes away from us, probably less at 7 in the morning. The marketing team knew exactly where I lived as they had been over for drinks a few months prior — down an alleyway with only one exit, and up a singular stairwell. No side exits. We needed time to break down our apartment, but we had no idea how much time we actually had.

I fumbled through my cabinets in a rush, unsure of what I was really looking for. Took a deep breath, brought myself under control, and started working through what I had to do. What do I have that I don't want stolen?

Cash. Put ten grand in my backpack and hid another ten on my girlfriends body. They don't know her. We can send her down the stairwell and out the alleyway first. If they're waiting in the alley, she can walk right by them, leave, and let us know.

Passport.
Two days of clothes.
Notebooks.

James was securing his computers and wiping hard drives, shredding and flushing documents. They could show up at the door any second, and we can't have any information or money vulnerable to theft if that happens. Girlfriend leaves to go to work. Makes it out fine. No one in the alley, she says.

Deferred Admission

I check my phone. Easily a hundred missed messages and calls, starting from three in the morning all the way until now. Michael. His wife. James's girlfriend. Random other team members. All telling us to GTFO, they were coming for us.

Michael's messages shed a tiny bit of clarity on the situation. They realized the money had been frozen two nights ago, and waited outside Michael's house for him to come home. He was at my house late that night and they left before he got there. The second night they were waiting when he arrived. Knocked on his door and barged in the second he opened — the four team members plus four hired muscle. Made him and his wife sit on the couch, took their phones. Beat them. Made him give them all the crypto he had on any computer in the house. Not much. Less than 20 Bitcoin and a few thousand of our own coin in total. Apparently, this was a multi-hour ordeal, since they didn't know how to run the wallet programs themselves and made Michael do it for them. Michael told them they were wasting their time; the money was with James. They said they'd go to our place next. The woman team member threatened him with a knife — a much more serious crime than just beating them, according Chinese law. Her husband, one of the team members and a former cop, knew this and stopped her.

A former cop. Is that relevant? James and I were debating. Does he have any pull? Can he read our messages live? If our passports show up at a hotel or anywhere, can he track us?

Still needing a few more minutes to finish cleaning up his computers and booking an immediate flight to the US, James asked for a favor. Would I make coffee? Sure. Got right on it. Slammed the coffee and prepared to leave. He decided once we were in a car that we should be fine, and I wouldn't need to accompany him to the airport. I could go find my dad at his hotel. I hadn't explained to him what was going on yet, I just sent a text message:

We need to meet immediately. Don't leave hotel. Will be up there ASAP.

James and I called a car and left the apartment cautiously. Down the pitch-black stairwell from the third floor to ground level, taking care to shine a flashlight in the small communal areas and potential blind spots before moving past them. The alley itself only has one main gate in and out, about 100 yards from our building's front door. That 100-yard stretch has a handful of small offshoots — side alleys leading to other buildings — that we'd have to pass carefully. We walked through the alley ready for a fight, but there was none. Made it out onto the street and into the car safely. After we drove a few blocks I got out and switched cars, then drove up to the hotel to find my dad. I explained the situation to him. Upon receiving my text, he had understood the meaning that was missing in the brevity and had been checking immediate flights out of the country. I wasn't ready for that yet, though. I had another coffee, still no food. Mind going at the speed of light, absolutely wired. I'm fueled by coffee and hate, like what's written on those t-shirts marketed to veterans.

While I was at the hotel Michael called me, frantic. Told me to come to his house immediately. They're coming back. I wasn't sure why he didn't just flee his apartment. The only response I got for asking was increasingly frantic phone calls ordering me to come at once. I suppose after what he and his wife had gone through, they wanted physical backup before they'd step outside. My dad and I got a cab to his house. We got in his car with him and his wife and we headed out. The thugs hadn't come back to his place yet, and he wasn't going to wait for them. We drove to the police station to follow up on their report from earlier. Then we went to the hospital so they could have doctors sign off on legal certificates documenting their wounds from the beating. The entire ride there Michael doesn't stop screaming about the threat being at large and mocking his wife about her driving skills. They were both beaten up pretty badly. They'd have to spend most of the afternoon in the hospital. Michael said he couldn't go home that night or check into a hotel since foreigners checking into hotels would register with the police, and he was afraid they'd be tipped off. I told him I'd take care of it while they were at the hospital.

My dad and I decided that once Michael was setup to be safe, we'd leave Shanghai so I could lay low. Knowing that I'd want more than one or two days of clothes, I decided to go back to my apartment and grab some more things. But there was a chance I'd find some uninvited guests there. Before heading back to my apartment my dad wanted to grab an advantage — a metal pipe, a baseball bat. I had to explain to him that in China if we beat the attackers up, even in self-defense, it wouldn't end well for us.

We took the subway back to my apartment and got out a few blocks away, deliberately walking about 50 yards apart so my dad could watch if anyone reacted oddly to seeing me. As we got to my street we split and walked the full length of the street, one on each side, checking every car and assessing every person we saw. Nothing. Checked every corner on our way down my alley. Slowly we worked our way up the stairs to my front door, hyper-sensitive to every sound and every blind corner on the way up. It didn't look like anyone had been there in the last two hours since I left. We go in, all clear. My dad went back to the alleyway to watch for any activity while I ripped through the apartment. Grabbed some extra clothes, set up an old iPhone as a makeshift security camera, and headed back to the hotel.

As we walked out of the alley and onto the street, I realized the guy who just passed me in the direction of my house was staring at me. I turned around. He stopped and turned around too. Still staring. He had gloves on. It was summer and 105 degrees outside, why does he have gloves on? I watched him watch me walk away.

We went back to the hotel and my dad talked to the desk manager. Since he is a frequent guest, he managed to get an upgrade to a two-bedroom apartment suite. Our new safehouse. I waited for Michael and his wife to come in the parking garage, snuck them directly up to the room and avoided registration. Probably unnecessary. But we were not taking any risks.

Once Michael was there, he got on the phone with a long-time partner of his, the owner of an exchange in Shanghai. He frequently acted as counsel to Michael. He was also a potential target of the marketing team. His thinking was that the likelihood of any further criminality was unlikely, and they were probably either already in police custody or already outside the country, on the run. If they happened to still be in Shanghai, they were in hiding. The fact that they'd already acted so belligerently and now had their backs to the wall did mean they were liable to act even crazier, though, so we should all take extra precaution. It was time to get out of town for a while.

Later that night someone from the marketing team — the woman who threatened Michael with the knife — called Michael's wife. They talked and argued on the phone for over an hour. When the call was finally over, Michael's wife relayed the contents to us: The woman finally admitted that they had embezzled the money, but that was beside the point, and in a surprisingly bold move, the woman's purpose in calling was to demand, *it's our money now, and we want it back!*

I decided it wasn't necessary to leave the country entirely. I'd just go into the interior, to central-southern China, and pass a few days waiting for updates from those on the ground in Shanghai. If James, Michael, and I were all out of Shanghai, there shouldn't be anyone else in danger. Michael hadn't decided where he'd go yet, so he stayed in the safehouse for a few more days. My dad and I flew to Chengdu first thing

Lashing Out

the next morning. Before that, I wanted to see my girlfriend one more time before going into hiding, so I invited her over to the safehouse too. It was the first time she met any member of my family, or that they were even made aware of her existence. Quite the occasion.

When I boarded the plane to Chengdu the next morning, I sent a quick message to Charlie in the US to let him know what was happening. My tone was partially serious and partially boastful. All our childhood we'd watched gangster movies and thought it would be cool to live like that. Now I (sort of) was. I don't wish any harm on anyone, and it's horrible that my friends got hurt, but I was genuinely enjoying myself. After months of near directionless wandering while enjoying unreal success, this was a pure, straight-up adrenaline rush. I was made for this kind of situation. I am at peak, flawless performance under this kind of pressure. Nothing else can approximate it.

I let my guard down once in Chengdu. No news came out of Shanghai for the first two days. Chengdu is the hip-hop epicenter of China, so I decompressed by hanging out with my local rapper friends, who I'd met by chance on previous trips. The slow, cozy pace of life in Chengdu took most of the edge off the last 24 hours. We spent whole afternoons sitting in People's Park smoking cigarettes and drinking tea, followed by hot pot and a night in the clubs. All the more enjoyable for being accompanied by varying degrees of local celebrity. But I couldn't lose myself in Chengdu's famous "*yanglao*" lifestyle (an approximately more graceful term for "retirement"), as the episode unfolding in Shanghai, and online, beckoned for my attention again.

People in our online community were beginning to sense something was wrong. Rumors were emerging in chatrooms, but there was no one taking the lead on any sort of public response. No one wanted to do so without Michael's instruction, but Michael was nowhere to be found.

The public community had yet to hear what happened. The big investors all had a chance to speak with Michael, though, and were mobilizing all their resources to protect him. Eventually I found out from his wife that he'd flown to Israel. We had some big Israeli backers, and they went ballistic when they heard about the situation, immediately flying him out and putting him under protection of the IDF. My first connection with Michael after fleeing Shanghai was when he sent me a picture of himself standing between two IDF soldiers with machine guns. *They're making sure I'm very safe here*, he told me.

Frankly, it wasn't really necessary and there wasn't much they could do, but it was an impressive response.

The Western marketing firm reached out to me to start developing a public response. It had to be done, and if Michael wasn't going to lead it then they would. Michael's wife orchestrated coordination with the new Chinese marketing team under her command. Honestly, I know nothing about public relations or law, but everyone was saying we need to be very careful with what we say, and that sounded reasonable. We worked hard to put together a response plan with multiple

Lashing Out

teams acting together. The releases went out. All the major crypto forums and chatrooms were shocked. Our own community was shocked that such a horrible thing would happen. The wider crypto community, cynically, was shocked that we'd lie so blatantly for attention. Whatever. Then Michael decided it was time to break radio silence.

He hated our response. We were all idiots. Insubordinate idiots, apparently. This was not how you respond to this kind of event and we should know better. Why were we worried about careful wording? He immediately went into all the chatrooms and went off on unrestrained tirades. We tried to moderate him. He got even angrier. It didn't help that his version of the story changed every time he told it. He wasn't lying, at least not intentionally, his mind just doesn't care about details.

After four days in Chengdu, Michael's wife told me it was safe to go back to Shanghai. There was no word on the marketing team's whereabouts, but they hadn't tried anything new and I could tell they hadn't been to my apartment, since I set up cameras.

I flew back to Shanghai and got very sick. I guess I caught something in Chengdu. Laying incapacitated in my bed in Shanghai, Michael sent me a message. He was going to tell the marketing team that I have the money they want. That way when they resurface and try to rob me, they can be arrested. I couldn't tell if he was joking or not, but either way he was safe in Israel. I wasn't. I went ballistic, screaming at Michael over the phone.

Deferred Admission

I've always felt my natural position in life is to be the right-hand man of a solid leader. Growing up, I repeatedly found myself in that position in the friend-group hierarchy. When I watched TV or movies, like *The Sopranos*, I identified more with Silvio than Tony. I never had a formal job title with the project in Shanghai. I was just working for Michael. I was great at it. Even after I'd fumbled the filter business and was more or less shot as Michael's go-to guy, my quick response and assistance with the home invasion had temporarily redeemed me. But after this episode and the way it was handled, I knew I couldn't stay in that role.

A few more weeks passed before I heard any update about the old marketing team. Once they found out all of their stolen funds had been frozen, they planned to rob Michael and force him to unfreeze the funds. They assumed they'd have all the money unfrozen and also get thousands of additional Bitcoin they were hoping he kept on his computer. Ride away into the sunset. But after they left the home invasion that night, still planning to go to my apartment to find James, they realized a few things: They'd only stolen less than 20 Bitcoin, which wouldn't make for much of a retirement fund for the four of them at current prices. None of the two million they originally stole was unfrozen, since Michael didn't control that in the first place, James did. But James held an intimidatingly large size advantage over them, and if they tried to "force" him to unfreeze the accounts, he'd probably beat them to death with both hands tied behind his back.

Lashing Out

So now they had just committed a home invasion, stolen a meager amount of money compared to what would be useful to them, and realized they were not going to get their accounts unfrozen. Meanwhile, the police were certainly called the minute they left Michael's house, and they were now Chinese nationals, still in China, with the police looking for them on assault and theft charges. They turned themselves in first thing in the morning.

The crypto market itself was dead now too. All the projects that had raised a hundred million from having a pretty website were bankrupt. Bitcoin was down to $6,000 after people had taken out second mortgages on their homes in January to buy at $20,000. Not a single new project that had come out in the last year delivered on anything. No one was raising any new money through ICOs. Any interest Hudson and I had in the new coin business was gone. The party was over.

I briefly considered continuing to work at the project in a more formal fashion. I went to the new marketing office and met with the team under Michael's wife. She eventually arrived at the office with her new bodyguards. We talked. She'd take me on in a formal position, but I was expected to come into the office every day, 9 to 5, for $1,500 a month. Shanghai local salary. Not what I was used to. The bubble spoiled me. I was done with the project. I'd been there for exactly one year.

All the stress, all the high-speed action movie maneuvering we'd done turned out to be unnecessary – in retrospect. In reality, operating under uncertainty, and with any possibility that the threat was still at-large, we acted 100%

correctly. We did what was necessary to be safe. Still, it was funny to think about.

Chapter 20

It's Been a Slow Year

> "Used my other hand to feel my elbow. That's weird, I remember there being a bone right there."

It was now July 2018. I had been in China by myself for just over a year at this point. After the recent experience, I decided it was time to go back to the United States and visit my friends and family for the first time since I'd left. I brought my girlfriend. It was her first time in the States and we had a great trip. I'd seen my immediate family a handful of times in the past year, but I hadn't seen most of my friends for a full year, quite a switch from seeing them almost every single day for over a decade. I was extremely happy. But I could also tell that I wasn't one of them anymore. A lot had happened in a year. The separation, the intensity of my experiences versus theirs, gave me a whole different perspective. I was simply on a different frequency. This would only get more pronounced in the future.

Deferred Admission

The one friend who I didn't feel increasingly separated from was Charlie. He was the only other one who didn't go to college. When I moved to Shanghai, he moved to New York and in early 2018, he started his own company with his freshman year college roommate (unlike me, he did go to *one* year of college, a man of letters). Recently they'd created a lending interface for a certain crypto project. It did heavy volume and they caught the attention of venture capital, securing significant funding just before I came back to the US. Where raising funds through the ICO market had collapsed, venture capital was still active, and they did not miss out on the opportunity.

  I got to see Charlie at home. We talked about all of our experiences over the last year. He said he was going to have to pull my passport after what happened recently with the home invasion. I appreciated the concern. I told him I was basically unemployed at this point. He offered I could join his new business. With the new funding, they wanted to expand, and he hoped I could promote their product in China. We'd work out the details once I was back. But he had other business to take care of first — namely, moving out of his crappy Lower East Side studio and getting himself a nicer place. He found an apartment right on Union Square. New company headquarters for the next year. The building only begrudgingly let him in. They weren't excited about having a 20-year-old college dropout as a tenant. Who cares, green is green and in is in.

  I got back to China just in time to celebrate my 19th birthday. My girlfriend bought me a motor scooter as a present.

It's Been a Slow Year

On the day of my birthday, I went out to lunch with a friend. After he left, I went to get coffee on my new scooter. Came into a corner too fast, jammed the brake mid-turn, and the scooter came right out from under me. Slid across the street into the sidewalk. Slowly I sat up, disoriented. Elbow hurts. Couldn't really move my arm. Used my other hand to feel my elbow. That's weird, I remember there being a bone right here.

My right elbow swelled to the size of a baseball and I'm not really sure where the bone went. There's an old man standing over me, pointing.

Too fast, too fast, he says in Chinese.

Thanks, I got that. Can you help me call an ambulance?

Too fast, too fast.

I call myself an ambulance.

After ten minutes it finally came. And it immediately went. Blew right past me. Eventually it made its way back. Another ten minutes to the ER. First thing when I get off the ambulance, someone looks me over and asks:

Are you ok to walk?

Yes.

Did you bring your wallet?

Uh, yeah.

Ok, go pay first.

I stumbled over to the cashier with my right arm locked at a 90-degree angle, dripping blood, swelling elbow approaching small balloon size. Took care of the fee, saw the doctor, and got an X-ray. Part of my elbow made its way up by my bicep. Not where it was supposed to be. They said I needed surgery but recommended I do it at a Western hospital. If I got admitted to the Chinese hospital, I would be kept for a week while they scheduled a surgery. A Western hospital would have me out within a day. Doctor recommended an "American" hospital nearby. I made an appointment.

Chinese hospitals don't give painkillers stronger than ibuprofen, so I spent the next two days with nothing but ibuprofen and some gauze wrapped so tight around my arm that my hand became paralyzed. Went back to the emergency room. *Oh, whoops, that is way too tight, sorry.* I went to my appointment at the "American" clinic and they scheduled a surgery for the weekend. How odd — they said the clinic's surgeons are all Americans but here was the same Chinese doctor from the public ER saying he's going to do my surgery. And wow, look at this bill. Wait a second…

As my insurance was denying the pre-authorization claim to do the surgery at the "American" clinic, the realization slowly came to me that they were trying to scam me. Why would the Chinese public hospital doctor follow me to do the surgery at the private clinic? Why was there a $2,000 "new patient registration fee" charge coming up at the clinic? F*ck me.

I got a recommendation for a proper Western hospital from a doctor friend. They saw me and scheduled a surgery for a week later. Surgery shouldn't have been delayed this long, but permanent damage to your arm isn't *too* likely, they said. I spent another week on ibuprofen, trying as hard as I could not to move my dominant arm whatsoever. I began to realize, painfully, that you move your dominant arm instinctively quite a lot. Finally had the surgery with no complications and began the road to recovery.

Once my surgery was done, I started marketing Charlie's products. Moderately successful, I gained them something of a following but nothing huge. He let me go after a month. Even with moderate success in my promotion, they had to cut back spending given the state of the market. No hard feelings.

That was mid-October. Nothing of note happened between then and the following April. Seriously, it was the polar opposite of my previous year. I think balance had to be restored to the universe after the non-stop action of my first year in China, my first year out of high school. Crypto prices were crushed but I had made enough money to not feel any pressure to get a job. I semi-seriously considered becoming a barista at a friend's coffee shop. I invested in another friend's coffee shop. I traveled around China when my family came to visit. I very,

very briefly rejoined Michael's hardware team because I was so f*cking bored. That lasted a week and a half before I quit again.

    I honestly have a hard time remembering what exactly I did on a day-to-day basis during that period. I only remember occasionally traveling for a weekend or a couple weeks here and there with family. Outside of travel, I must have just been waiting for the bubble to come back and carry me away again.

    I spent the last two weeks of March 2019 traveling through China with my family. We went to Guangzhou and while there, Charlie called me. He had an idea for a new product. He wanted me to be a part of it and fly to New York as soon as I could to help develop it. I told him I'd be over as soon as I wrapped up the trip. My family went back to the States, I spent two or three days in Shanghai with my girlfriend, and then I flew to New York to start working with Charlie and, hopefully, reclaim my fast-paced crypto bubble lifestyle.

Chapter 21

New York – A New Start

"We took a few blockchain beers for the road and walked back to Union Square."

I got to New York on the night of April 4th, grabbed a cab into town from Newark and arrived at Charlie's apartment just before midnight. Elevator doors opened directly into the main room. Charlie, Victor (his business partner/roommate) and a few guys I hadn't met were there, already drunk, blasting techno over the speaker system. Charlie handed me a beer and introduced me around. I tried to insist I just got off a 12-hour flight, didn't really want to get drunk. He couldn't understand my line of thinking.

The next day we were more on the same page. A decentralized finance ("DeFi") meetup was being held in Soho and Charlie and I wanted to go. Check out the New York crypto scene? Make some contacts? No. There were two running jokes at that point. 1) Blockchain beer. Meetups had free beer. You don't go to a meetup to meet people, or to learn something, but to get your blockchain beer. 2) Meetups had changed from attracting genuine hobbyists to insufferable grifters. We'd both been going to crypto meetups and conferences for over two years at this point. They stopped being interesting after the first few months. Everyone had been giving the same talk for years. The same inane, condescending garbage about how they were going to give a Bhutanese farmer the same financial capabilities as a Wall Street executive. Panelists who say their company is just oh so passionate about helping *Africa*. Talking about impoverished villagers in the developing world as an abstraction, a vaguely defined group in desperate need of millennials from Brooklyn to save them with blockchain. If only we could get them trading futures, surely their quality of life would skyrocket. Without fail, you will hear someone talk like this if you go to a blockchain meetup:

> *So you've got a rice farmer in Bhutan, right? And he's illiterate. Total f*ckin' idiot. And we're going to give him a computer, and with the computer he can trade futures on his rice using Ethereum. Hedge his exposure to the village market. Financial freedom, ever heard of it?*

Ok, maybe they're not that blunt. But that's how I hear it.

Outside of the speeches were the personas themselves. People who got mildly internet famous in the bubble took themselves very seriously. There's not a single person in the entire cryptocurrency space that claims a sub-C-Suite title. For people who don't have a specific company on which to hang their CEO/COO/Founder status, the slightly vague but equally prestigious "investor" or "fund manager" will do. Assets under management? Uh, we don't disclose that (around $2,000… family and friends).

At the meetup we made it a challenge — who could last the longest without laughing. Were we dicks? Sure… but we felt justified. The presentation was a panel comprised of the above $2,000-AUM fund manager type. Not even funny at first. No urge to laugh. Charlie started laughing just because he was trying not to. Victor and I nearly lost it. Then one of the panelists said it. *Cryptocurrency futures trading for Pakistani onion farmers.* We lost it. I was crying. If it wasn't a room full of people from Brooklyn we'd almost certainly have been escorted out. They tried their best to ignore us. How was nobody else laughing? No, seriously, how are people still attending this exact same talk after three years? Why can't people just say they want to make a financial product without feeling the need to package it as a charity? We took a few blockchain beers for the road and walked back to Union Square.

We started getting serious about the new project — the reason I'd come out in the first place. Charlie explained the concept to me: derivative markets on the blockchain. Allow users to take leveraged positions on real-world assets, all denominated in cryptocurrency. A big deal, if done right. He had the general idea but wanted me to help figure out how to set up the markets to be profitable. While I worked on that, Victor would code the actual program.

I worked a bit on my part but spent most of the month talking through our future plans with Charlie: Whether or not we'd stay in New York. Whether or not to raise more capital. He and I are both very effective workers when we — separately — put our minds to something. But we have a risk, when together, to be totally incapable of taking anything seriously if we don't severely discipline ourselves. Everything's a big joke. It's not so good for business. It's a lot of fun, though, if that counts for anything.

The month went by quickly and the product was almost finished. We prepared to release it. We'd limit the release to select locations outside of the US. I'd go promote it in China as a test run to see what kind of attention it would gain.

Before I left New York, Charlie and I made a plan. He was sick of New York, but not ready to leave the United States entirely like I had. We considered going for a bigger fundraising round and set our sights on a 30 million dollar raise. Switch from Union Square to the Hollywood Hills. Why not? Other businesses were still raising that much money from venture capital without a working product. Meanwhile Charlie had already released a suite of massively popular products before this current one, which we were sure would be a hit.

My last night in town we accompanied a friend on a blind date we'd set up for him. Japanese food. We told him about our plan, drowning his cozy dinner for two with talk about fundraising for blockchain-based options trading. He thought we had our sights set too high. Buzzkill. A 100% correct assessment of the fundraising landscape in crypto at the time, but we didn't want to hear it. I flew back to Shanghai the next morning.

As soon as I got back to Shanghai the plan began to change. I promoted the new product as best I could, but it was slow to gain traction. Eventually we got one user who put a decent amount of money through it. Charlie and Victor decided they needed to spend some time refiguring and refining the product then re-release. Meanwhile our fundraising and location plans were unclear. Charlie and Victor took a trip to Los Angeles to look at properties. I helped Charlie put together some materials for pitching the raise. A week or two passed when I couldn't get a hold of him at all. I was concerned whether or not the plan would come through. He finally called me. He was in London.

After looking at homes and office space throughout Los Angeles, they'd gone up to meet with the current investors in San Francisco. The market, even with venture capital, had turned down. There was little interest in another raise. Maybe we could do 10 million if we sold most of the company, but 30 million was out of the question. Charlie decided to forget about a raise and focus on making the most with the money we still had, which was just over a million. He also decided that to do this, for this product, we'd have to leave the United States for a more favorable jurisdiction. This kind of product simply wouldn't work out of the US. You can either neuter the features of the project and destroy its value or try to game extremely complex regulations — a game you will not win. That's why he was in London. Just got there after spending a few days in the

Isle of Man. Told me they'd be in Taipei next week and I should meet them there. They wanted to look at options in Taipei and then Hong Kong. I was in Bangkok at the time visiting a friend, so I went back to Shanghai and started getting things in order for Taipei — real estate agents, the hotel, all my relevant business contacts from the bubble. I wanted to show them a good time. I had a strong preference that the business be moved to Asia. No interest in Europe.

I met them in Taiwan and played host for a few days. We looked at houses in the mountains surrounding the city. Office space around the Taipei 101. Unfortunately, the consultants weren't throwing any parties this time. I hadn't heard from them in a while, and wondered if they went away with the bubble.

I was still able to introduce them to all my active contacts, though. One of the guys from the exclusive after-after-party of December 2017 had been pretty successful, even after the bubble ended. His company took over an entire building and made it the first fully-crypto office building in Taipei. They were having a private party to celebrate. I wasn't close to him, but another one of my contacts put us on the invite list. A nice afternoon of day drinking and networking. All the same faces from before were there, including the consultants. Still around after all. There were models at the party, he must have learned to do this from them.

We flew from Taipei to Hong Kong, hoping to have a similar trip. Spend a few days there. Get a good feel for the place and understand our options. We got in on Sunday around

New York – A New Start

noon and drove to our hotel in Central. The street in was blocked. Oh right, I forgot, riots. I had been in Seoul during pro/anti-government protests, where tens of thousands rallying peacefully would create congestion. But this was peak Hong Kong riot season. This was mayhem and felt out of control. In fact, the day we got there was the day they started indiscriminately beating people in the subway station. We rushed through the crowds to get to the bars. The hour and 20-minute flight from Taipei had drained us and we needed a drink. The rioters were making it difficult.

Sunday means that the bars are filled with Filipina migrant workers. Maids. It's their day off. The holy day. So they go to the bar to find Johns. Semi-pros — if they like you it's free. Being Hong Kong, the Johns are 60-year-old British and Australian men. There to party. They gave us mean looks when we got to the bar, irritated at having the spotlight taken off them by a few young bucks. We meant no harm. Just wanted our drinks. The girls are all theirs.

We bar hopped and drank through the whole night, making our way from dodgy Wan Chai to the more age-appropriate party central of Lan Kwai Fong. Woke up the next morning so hungover we went straight to the airport. They flew to New York; I flew to Shanghai. Hong Kong ruined in the first 18 hours. It can be a dark place.

Hong Kong was going to be too expensive for the business, anyway, and didn't offer any advantages that Taipei lacked. I assumed we were set on Taipei. Everything was in motion. Both Charlie and I would go back home for a visit before we made the move. As usual, the plans changed quickly.

Chapter 22

European Vacation

> "If the Isle of Man was Heaven on earth, Malta was Hell. It took just over 48 hours to realize this."

I'd gotten engaged to my girlfriend in the beginning of July before going to Taipei. We went back to my hometown and announced it to family and friends. I bought her a ring. Talking through the Taipei plans with Charlie, I noticed he seemed hesitant. In the last few days before I returned to Shanghai, he finally let me know the new plan: Isle of Man and Malta. These two places had the best possible regulatory environment for our product. Isle of Man was home to online gambling giants like PokerStars and had a straightforward, relatively low-barrier-to-entry system for regulating that kind of business. Malta, even more so than Taiwan, wanted to become "Crypto Island" or even "Crypto Nation", and was building out regulatory frameworks to be as inviting and friendly as possible to cryptocurrency businesses.

Charlie wanted to move there to build the business. He'd already bought tickets. We'd stay in the Isle through October at a minimum and check out Malta as well if we had time. I wasn't surprised that plans changed again, but I was a bit annoyed at the prospect of going to Europe. I'd never been before and just assumed I'd hate it. He told me to go as soon as possible.

I thought "as soon as possible" would be a month, at minimum. There were engagement celebrations to attend in my fiancée's hometown in China. I had to get a new passport. My fiancée had to get visas for the UK and EU. Everything ended up being taken care of in just under a month's time. I took her on a little trip to Chengdu, then flew directly to the Isle of Man. Directly from China of course meaning, first to Abu Dhabi, then Manchester, then the Isle. It's not easy to get there.

We landed in the morning on September 23rd. Charlie had already been there for over a month, Victor around three weeks. The lease on the apartment in New York was up and they were fully moved out. Before I got there, they'd already established a local company and office space, and made government regulatory contacts. Nowhere on earth is more business friendly than the Isle of Man.

To be clear, I am a huge buyer of the Isle of Man. Friendly people, nice enough weather, beautiful scenery. Regulations are straightforward and easy to understand. The government collaborates with you in person to make your business work. Our office was a couple rooms, newly renovated, in a castle just outside the capitol. We were renting a house right on the beach in Castletown, on the south side of the island. Five bedrooms, all three couples living in it together. We three guys got up at six or seven every morning, went to the office, worked hard all day and came back around seven or eight at night with dinner waiting. I thought I'd dislike the UK for some reason, but I discovered I loved it. Charlie and I would go to the pub after dinner and have a few pints while discussing the business. The lifestyle was perfect, better than anything during the bubble a year and a half before. It lasted for four days.

On the morning of the fourth day, Charlie let me know a meeting had been scheduled with the financial and gambling commissions so they could determine whose jurisdiction our product fell under. He and I would go to the capitol for the meeting while Victor continued coding.

It was critical that we be regulated as a gambling product. If we were a gambling product, we didn't even need a gambling license to operate our business from the Isle of Man. So long as our servers that handled the actual gambling transactions were located outside the Isle, we could have an office and employees, incorporate and run the business from inside the Isle. If we were a financial product, on the other hand, it would destroy the business. Regulating a financial product in the Isle of Man is maybe only slightly less complicated than regulating it anywhere else in the world. Compliance is expensive and the regulations are complex. We needed simplicity and couldn't afford much in the way of legal fees.

Deferred Admission

We got to the capitol on time for our 9 a.m. meeting. Dressed sharp. We were led into the meeting room and another eight or so men came in from various government offices. My first time meeting any of them. Charlie was familiar with a few. We explained our product and answered questions. Charlie had told me previous meetings were easygoing. Not this time. These guys were stern. The head of the financial regulatory body interrupted us as we offered a demo of the product. *I don't want to be burdened with that information.* Meeting was called to a close. One of the guys Charlie was familiar with took us aside.

> *Seems like it's going to have to be a financial product, legally. Meeting was called off because they know you guys don't want that, but if they see more it'll be a done deal. You still have room to tinker with it now, see if you can come up with a way to change it to be a gambling product.*

We couldn't really change it. It was perfect. To be a gambling product, per what we discovered to be the local definition, there would have to be rigid, predefined "odds" for each trade executed on our platform. Like you're sitting at the blackjack table. But there was no way to implement that without entirely overhauling the platform, and in the process ruining it. The entire selling point was allowing people to get dynamic exposure to real-world assets with their crypto. Not to mention we weren't interested in trying to play "the house" with this product. The entire planned legal structure in the Isle was based on us being regulated as a gambling project. F*ck.

140

European Vacation

    Charlie and I were cool at first, maybe slightly disconcerted. We strolled through the capitol, got a coffee, headed back to the office. Victor asked how the meeting went. Great. I tried to get to work marketing, but Charlie told me to hold off while he considered the regulatory status. We both stewed on it the rest of the day.

    What happened next was a result of immaturity and, in my opinion, killed the business right there and then, just four days after I'd moved myself and my fiancée across the world to build the company.

    Charlie and I were each individually overthinking the impact of the meeting on our status in the Isle. Then we started talking to each other about it and got increasingly worked up. We decided we had to leave the Isle. Not next week, not after attempting another meeting or tweaking the product, not even after sleeping on it for one night. Now. Tonight. Fly to Malta as soon as possible, the rules should be better there. Looking back on it, I'm embarrassed how wound up I got and how poorly I made decisions. It's insane. But that's how it happened. We packed up all the office equipment as fast as possible, drove home, and told the girls to pack their bags. My fiancée had gotten an EU visa for Malta in China, but we now realized there was a designated start date and she couldn't enter for another month. How were we going to deal with that? *We'll figure it out later, have to go now* (why? how?). My fiancée and I flew to London that night. She'd worked there a couple years earlier and wanted to show me the city. I'd promised her I'd go with her, and it seemed like that had to be done now. We'd stay for the weekend. Everyone else flew to Malta the next morning.

Europe (including the UK) is stupid expensive. I think I spent over $2,000 just on lodging and flights in and out for our three days in London. It was a mix of a great weekend and the most soul-crushingly stressful few days of my life. I've never been so angry or stressed than I was those few days. How was I going to deal with my fiancée if I had to go to Malta and she couldn't go yet? Could I postpone going to Malta for the time being? Charlie said he needed me there, then he didn't, then it would be best if I was there but it's up to me. We were both under a lot of pressure. He'd left his girlfriend and her mom (who had also tagged along for the whole IOM trip) at the rental house in Castletown. They were also Chinese and without EU visas entirely.

The whole situation was preposterous. Just silly. I don't know if it came from our subconscious, our innate character as troublemakers looking to cause a scene, or if it came from our pride, looking to play-act important businessmen with big problems. Or maybe we're just f*cking idiots. I'm undecided, pick whatever you think fits.

At least London was nice. London being beautiful is probably the sole thing that kept me from a full-blown heart attack. Made me wish I was born British.

After running through every possible plan, we decided my fiancée would fly back to the Isle and stay with Charlie's girlfriend and her mom. It made me uneasy, but the Isle of Man

European Vacation

is Heaven on earth so at least I wasn't concerned for their safety. I flew to Malta on October 1st.

If the Isle of Man was Heaven on earth, Malta was Hell. It took just over 48 hours to realize this. At first I was mesmerized by the historical aspect of the place. Warm weather, Italian food, and it looked like you were living in ancient Rome. What's not to love? I'll tell you what's not to love: Horrible service; getting heat stroke if you go outside for more than 10 minutes in October; spending a hundred Euros a day to eat raw pork in a dirty alleyway while you swat away an infinite stream of flies. There are no nice grocers, just low-quality supermarkets and seemingly cute little family run markets selling rotten produce. If you turn on a flashlight at night in what's supposed to be your newly renovated, modern apartment, you'll see approximately 100 mosquitos on the wall six inches above your pillow. They buzz in your ear all night, every night. For some reason, if you go out before eight in the morning, the only people in the street are fresh off the boat African refugees who follow you home. The list goes on endlessly.

We stayed the first week in an Airbnb on the beautiful Sliema waterfront. By beautiful I mean it was a dump. While the UK surprised me with how nice it was, Malta was exactly what I originally expected Europe to be and I hated it. Horrible but expensive restaurants. Dirty. I've said too much on this, though. There's an easier way for me to explain how horrible it was: For the first time ever, I bought myself a pack of cigarettes.

We had work to do though. When I arrived in the Isle, a month of work in building government contacts and a legal structure for the business had already been done. Now we had to recreate that in Malta. Trouble is, Malta wasn't as open as the Isle of Man. Our first step was to inquire about the Maltese "Global Residence Program" that would allow us to properly base there. Becoming residents of Malta would provide a few big benefits — namely, the ability to legally prove we were *not* residents of the United States, which was potentially necessary to operate the business. Also, by becoming residents of Malta, we would be EU residents, and could ultimately live wherever we liked within the EU, with the business officially in Malta as needed. We set up a meeting with KPMG.

    I wrote the last paragraph and now I'm laughing. "We had work to do." It's true, we did. But any sense of direction or discipline or focus was totally obliterated after leaving the UK. It's what Michael must have felt like in late bubble period. Trying to do a million things at once, unable to articulate the goal of any of the million things. It was near impossible to work there. You felt sick and sluggish from the food. Didn't help that we were constantly smoking and drinking. No sleep, too many mosquitos. No office, just working on laptops in the living room of an Airbnb. There was only one good stretch of work done after getting to Malta. Sometime in the first week. Charlie and I sat down with our computers, a pack of cigarettes, and two bottles of wine. Didn't get up for six hours. Carried conversations across tens of Reddit boards and even more Telegram chatrooms simultaneously, trying to gain a following for the project. Still didn't get any users.

European Vacation

Tried to lighten the mood one night. We took a cab across the island to what was supposed to be the most beautiful beach on Malta. It was underwhelming. There was a small burger restaurant. Charlie and I plopped down there and were served disgusting burgers by Eastern Europeans and laughed our asses off to cope. Went to the nightlife district on the way back. St. Julian's. Bars packed to the brim with 15-year-old Russians on vacation. Sleaziest place I've ever been in my life, and if you've read this far, you know that is saying something.

We were miserable. Got sick, even worse. At least my fiancée was having a good enough time in the Isle of Man. Charlie and I decided to fly back to be with them. Not like we were doing any work, anyway. Our plane got delayed and the Malta airport is, surprise surprise, a dump. He left and went back to his apartment. I stuck with it. Flying in Europe is a real treat. They only have budget airlines where the pilot's a 22-year-old and you get crammed into unimaginably tiny seats that don't recline. Get excited that tickets are just 50 Euro, until you realize each piece of baggage larger than a fanny pack is an extra 100 Euro. Not checked through to your destination.

I spent two or three weeks back in Castletown with my fiancée. A great time, especially after Malta. The contrast of going from Hell back up to Heaven was strong. I worked with scattered focus from the rental home. We had no more business in the Isle of Man. Guess I'm a digital nomad.

Charlie was spiraling deeper into Hell in Malta. He got an apartment the first week we were there. Alone in it now. Can't sleep until daybreak because there's only one exit in and out of the building, one door to his fourth-floor apartment, so in the event of any emergency whatsoever, he's easily screwed. And every time he leaves the house, he has to juke through alleyways to lose the various African and Middle Eastern youth tailing him. Someone's dealing drugs just across the street all through the night. Cherry on top.

My fiancée's EU visa was about to be valid. I wasn't excited at the prospect of taking her to Malta, but I was still convinced we had work to do, and I'd already paid for the Airbnb for the whole month of November. We flew down there on Halloween. Things went downhill very quickly.

I've always hated Airbnb, but I didn't want to sign a lease or pay a minimum of 300 Euro a night for a hotel, so we had no choice. As usual, it was a dump and nothing like the pictures. Small, cheap piece of shit, I'm paying $1,300 for the month. Lucky me, one door in and out just like Charlie. First day there, two men walk in unannounced. They had the key. *We're the... uh... cleaning staff. Sorry.* News comes out that there are severe, violent refugee riots going on near the airport. Situation around our apartment not much different. On the third or fourth day, a car outside Victor's apartment got firebombed. Ok, we're done. We flew back to China the next day. I knew I'd hate Europe.

Chapter 23

Tired of Taipei

"... they make sure to tell me my Chinese sounds just like a Chinese person. It's not meant as a compliment."

Charlie left Malta with us and headed to Shanghai. Victor went back to America. It was clear the business was shot. We spent two weeks in Shanghai discussing what to do next. Charlie still wanted to set up shop in Taipei. We flew over, looked at more houses, and applied for the "Entrepreneurship Visa" on the basis that we had received venture capital investment. This would make us residents of Taiwan. The application was approved. We found a unique townhouse on the side of Elephant Mountain, just off downtown. Four floors and a garage, on the side of the hill surrounded by jungle, overlooking the Taipei 101 for $3,000 a month. Had a koi pond. Charlie had to have it.

While Charlie was committing to Taipei by becoming a resident and getting a house, I wasn't sure I wanted to move

Deferred Admission

there. We had no business plan, it would be a pain to move, and I liked Shanghai. Not to mention I'd been going to Taipei once every other month for the last two years. I was getting tired of it. Not outright sick of it, but the city aggravated a sort of bipolar relationship I have with it. Love/hate. It's a beautiful, unique city. Nowhere else quite like it. A true big city that feels as comfy as a village, surrounded by mountainous jungle on all sides. It sounds silly, but I was getting increasingly irate with the food situation there. It's one of the richest cities in the world, but if you look at their diet, you wouldn't think that. No meat (no, three slices of beef in a bowl of beef-noodle soup doesn't count). Taiwanese food is various little snacks and noodles. You go stall by stall in 110-degree heat to eat a hot bowl of soup noodles on a plastic stool, forever. Eventually you stop eating, not because you're full, but because you can't take it anymore. Western tourists love the "night market culture" but trust me when I say, if you actually live in Asia, the novelty of that stuff wears off very quickly. If I'm going out, I want to sit down in a chair, in an air-conditioned restaurant, and have a large serving of animal protein and fat. Your options for meat-heavy meals in Taiwan are limited to Korean BBQ, which is horribly overrated, hot pot, and low-quality Western restaurants. I was tired of it.

 Also, now that my Chinese is fluent and you can't tell I'm not Chinese without looking at my face, every time I open my mouth in Taiwan, they make sure to tell me my Chinese sounds just like a Chinese person. It's not meant as a compliment.

Tired of Taipei

With the house and residency set up in Taipei, the only thing left to focus on was developing a business plan. We had nothing. Demoralized after Europe. The overall business may have fallen apart because of decisions we made, but the product would have been doomed even if we'd done everything right. We'd been initiated into this industry in a market where as long as you got eyes on you, you got money. Didn't matter what you did, so long as you shipped some sort of product. That market was dead, though. The market that remained was reminiscent of the pre-bubble market. The ICO bubble boys had scattered like cockroaches when you turn on the lights, leaving only a relatively small group of hardcore believers behind. These remaining believers comprised a larger group than they did pre-bubble, but their money was focused into a select few projects, and they were almost all in the United States, meaning we couldn't allow them to use our product for legal reasons. Any and all remaining active marketing outlets were aimed at them. No one else was looking. It was over.

Knowing this, we had a hard time coming up with a new plan. Weren't eager to. We'd grown tired of the market ourselves. Why deal with the stress of flying all over Europe to obscure places so you can kind of sort of legally create a product that there's no market for anymore? Why restart the same process in Taipei?

The coronavirus scare was picking up steam fast in early February. After Chinese New Year, I went to Taipei two days before they shut down flights from the mainland to see Charlie and my dad, who was there on a business trip. We were both in a weird spot. We'd been in crypto for the last three and a half years, starting when we were 17 and 19, respectively. We'd both been through the insane bubble, experienced it from different perspectives, and had been at the top of the industry when everyone in the world was talking about it. After the euphoria ended, we kept trying to resuscitate it, and even had some moderate success. But that was temporary. It was done now. For good. We'd have to find something else to do.

Charlie suggested he may leave Taiwan and go back to America. As is apparently natural for me whenever I'm recently unemployed, I started thinking about getting involved in the coffee business. I left Taiwan on February 12th. I haven't seen Charlie, or any of my family, since. He did go back to the US. Both of us are still trying to make sense of our experience. Figure out what the hell we're supposed to do now. I still don't have an answer. My wife's pregnant, though, so I should probably get to it.

Chapter 24
Afterword

You Can Try This at Home

People tell me what I did was amazing, special… unique. It was unique. No one else had the experience I had. I question whether I'm special, though. I tend to think anyone could do this; they just choose not to. But maybe that they choose not to means that they can't. Don't have the disposition. I don't know. Why do I care, anyway?

The first few lines of the Eminem song *Role Model*, are playing over and over in my as I write this.

Okay, I'm going to attempt to drown myself.

You can try this at home.

You can be just like me.

Is this book a call to eschew college? To buck the traditional route of credentialism — striving for education and career in the United States — in order to take on obscene amounts of personal risk and blaze your own path?

Can you do what I did? If you can, is it even desirable?

I know I wouldn't have had it any other way. But I say that as someone who admits he's messed up in the head. Someone who turned 21 just the other day and feels he's already done everything, who's been on the brink of a heart attack from copious amounts of stress more than a few times before even turning 20, who can't relate to anyone he grew up with. Someone who, from the day he turned 18, was in a peer group whose members were, *at the youngest,* 10 years older than him.

I watched Bitcoin go from $200 to $20,000. I had a paper salary of $4,000 a month jump to $100,000 a month, all as a teenager months out of high school. You've read about the side trips though the Cambodian countryside, pitches at swanky homes of African oligarchs, and drunken lunches with Chinese industrialists. It feels like nothing I do will ever match, much less beat, the high I got from life in the year following high school. Could I be spoiled for life? How could I ever accept a normal job?

I feel like I've been pretty honest in detailing the last few years of my teens. I had some great times, but some clear low points as well. There is no attempt on my part to encourage or discourage anyone trying to imitate me. However, you've

You Can Try This at Home

heard the phrase "Be careful what you wish for, it might just come true." You think you understand it… but you don't. Be careful what you wish for.

For every bit of flashy and outrageously good times I had by taking this path, I've been bestowed an (at least) equal amount of mind-numbing stress, experience of failure, and hard lessons that I certainly wouldn't have had to deal with in college. You know what's a lot less fun than watching Bitcoin go from $200 to $20,000? Watching it plummet back to earth and stagnate, bringing your salary and lifestyle along with it.

But without these hard experiences there would be no maturation or lessons learned. Around the time I turned 20 and had some time to think about that first year out of high school, I wrote down some of the main lessons.

> *You will get carried away and not know it. I went from massive excitement over $4,000 to complete lack of respect for $300,000 in six months. You are high (as in, drug high) but don't know it, and planning is necessary beforehand. Plus you need the discipline to, in the midst of the high, execute the plan and say, OK, time to take some chips off the table.*

Good advice. If only I'd taken it myself, as my dad told me over and over throughout the course of the bubble to take chips off the table. Unfortunately, I'm just not that wise, and I need to touch the pan on the stove to know it's hot. Luckily I touched this pan when I was 18.

Deferred Admission

The interactions and experiences I had in 2017/18 made me very cynical about cryptocurrency. It was simply tiresome to deal with a never-ending stream of con artists trying to pick our pockets, then go to conferences to hear well-dressed conmen (marketers) give the same buzzword-laden speech over and over. Even as real, tangible progress in the technology was being made, I often couldn't see it from where I was standing, overwhelmed by the sheer amount of activity.

I think my cynicism was justified, but my analysis was wrong. In the last few chapters, I repeatedly referred to the cryptocurrency market as "dead" or otherwise finished. At the time, I really felt that way about the entire market. But now I've come to realize that what had died wasn't cryptocurrency as a technology, but the market environment that I was brought up in. The crazy times of 2016-2018 were gone, my attempts to resuscitate them aside. And since that was all I knew, I figured if it was done, crypto was done. Despite my lamentations about the prevalence of "marketing types" and scammers, my involvement in the space was nonetheless largely defined by interactions with them. I was never one of the original, technical-minded people myself, even if they took me under their wing. The bubble was a time of trying to find a place to fit crypto in the "real world" or, more accurately, the traditional business world, with people like me who could mesh with the technical types and business types alike trying to drive the evolution. It was also a sort of war between autists and sociopaths, the latter trying to claim ownership of the space over the former.

I'm not going to predict the future of cryptocurrency, of Bitcoin's price, or anything like that. Frankly, I'm still undecided on a lot of it. The only thing I can say is that every time I have to interact with a bank, I'm immediately reminded why I was bullish on Bitcoin in the first place. I still genuinely believe in Bitcoin. I'm sympathetic to the original ideology, and the experience of using it is incomparably better than dealing with a bank. It can only get better from here.

Made in the USA
Middletown, DE
06 November 2020